PENGUIN BOOKS

# THE LAW MACHINE

Marcel Berlins, a former practising lawyer and civil servant, is the author of several books on legal themes and has presented a number of television series, including *The Law Machine*. He now presents the BBC radio programme *Law in Action* and writes a weekly legal column in the *Guardian*.

Clare Dyer, a solicitor, is legal correspondent of the *Guardian* and of the *British Medical Journal*. She also writes on legal topics for a number of magazines. Together with Marcel Berlins, she is the author of *Living Together* (1982).

# The Law Machine

MARCEL BERLINS and
CLARE DYER

FIFTH EDITION

PENGUIN BOOKS

PENGUIN BOOKS

Published by the Penguin Group
Penguin Books Ltd, 27 Wrights Lane, London w8 5tz, England
Penguin Putnam Inc., 375 Hudson Street, New York, New York 10014, USA
Penguin Books Australia Ltd, Ringwood, Victoria, Australia
Penguin Books Canada Ltd, 10 Alcorn Avenue, Toronto, Ontario, Canada m4v 3b2
Penguin Books (NZ) Ltd, Private Bag 102902, NSMC, Auckland, New Zealand

Penguin Books Ltd, Registered Offices: Harmondsworth, Middlesex, England

First published in Pelican Books 1982
Second edition 1986
Third edition 1989
Reprinted in Penguin Books 1990
Fourth edition 1994
Fifth edition 2000
10 9 8 7 6 5 4 3 2 1

Set in 10/12.5 pt PostScript Adobe Minion
Typeset by Rowland Phototypesetting Ltd, Bury St Edmunds, Suffolk
Printed in England by Clays Ltd, St Ives plc

# Contents

# Introduction

The aim of this book is to explain, we hope clearly and entertainingly, how the machinery of justice – the law machine – actually works in practice. It is not designed to probe the content of particular laws, or to provide a guide to your rights. But laws and rights can only be properly understood if there is an appreciation of the legal process of which they form part. A law on its own is meaningless unless it can be channelled through an effective legal machinery.

The book arose originally from a London Weekend Television series *The Law Machine*, which was transmitted in 1983. For the first time on British television real lawyers – barristers and solicitors – and real judges appeared not just as interviewees or panellists, but doing their normal job. The series took as its starting point a fictitious motor accident in which a car driven by John Smith ran into a pedestrian, Anne Jones. It followed Smith through to his appearance at the Crown Court, where he was prosecuted for reckless driving, and then looked at Anne Jones's attempt to get compensation for her injuries in the High Court. The two trials on which the series focused were the most realistic ever staged on British television. Smith and Jones and the witnesses were played by actors, but the lawyers were practising barristers and solicitors treating the trial, and the conferences and negotiations leading up to it, just as they would have done in a real case. The judges were highly experienced, recently retired judges. The jury was chosen in the same way as a real jury. No part of the trials – including the jury's deliberations and verdict, and the judge's decision – was scripted. Nor were any of the meetings between the lawyers and their clients.

The book uses the staged trials as a useful device for explaining the way the criminal and the civil processes work. The book, however, deals with far more than the series was able to do in the relatively short time available.

The six years since the publication of the fourth edition has been an exceptionally active period in the development of the legal system, not least because of the radical reforms introduced by the Labour government since 1997. On almost every front there has been change, reassessment and new ideas. The legal profession has been shaken up, not always to its liking. The system of civil justice – the settlement of disputes – has been streamlined almost beyond recognition, and even its centuries-old vocabulary has been brought up to date. The funding of litigation has been drastically altered. 'Access to justice for all' has become the government's legal war-cry. The much-criticized criminal justice system, too, keeps trying to find new ways of adapting to the changing face of criminality, the views of successive Home Secretaries, and the need for fairness towards those caught up in it. A new generation of judges has emerged, with views more flexible and less hidebound than their older colleagues, and in general, there has been a move by the entire legal establishment towards a more open, modern approach. But doubts remain, covering every aspect of the workings of the law machine. Frantic activity doesn't always bring the results sought.

We thank all who gave of their time to read, and advise on, the text. In particular we are grateful to Owen Davies QC, of 2 Garden Court, Ian Walker, of Russell Jones & Walker, Mark Harper of Withers, Ann Flintham of the Magistrates' Association and Mike Wicksteed of the Lord Chancellor's Department. Thanks also to Professor Basil Markesinis, Director of the Institute of European and Comparative Law, Oxford University, for his encouragement.

We have described the system as at 15 April 2000, but we have tried also to signpost developments for the future.

To avoid awkwardness and the constant repetition of 'he or she' and 'his or her', we have used the male pronoun to include the female. The system we describe is that of England and Wales – Scotland and Northern Ireland have their own.

Marcel Berlins
Clare Dyer
April 2000

# CHAPTER I

# Justice for All?

In an average year Parliament passes between 45 and 60 new acts, some just a page or two, others running to over a hundred pages. Every year ministers and government departments make over two thousand new sets of rules and regulations which also have the full force of law. In hundreds of court cases every year judges interpret, restate and redefine the law. In the process new rights are created and new obligations and restrictions are imposed.

The ordinary citizen has only the vaguest notion of what the law expects of him and what it can do for him. Surveys show that not only are people largely ignorant of the legal remedies open to them, they are likely to be at a loss to know where to take a legal problem – or often even to identify it as a problem with a legal solution.

The English legal system has many shortcomings. Yet even an entirely fault-free system must be counted a failure if it doesn't reach a large proportion of those who need it. Access is the first weak point in the law machine.

## Access to the law

Where do people take their legal problems? It depends. Certain types of problem are identified in the public mind with solicitors. Well over 90 per cent of house-buyers, for instance, consult solicitors. Criminal charges and divorce are also normally seen as matters needing legal help and advice. So are making a will and dealing with the estate of someone who has died. But many essentially legal problems rarely come to solicitors: whether or not someone qualifies for a social security benefit, for example, and what to do if benefit is refused. The problem – if it is seen as capable of a solution at all – will not be seen as a legal one.

Even someone whose problem is more obviously a legal one – for example, a tenant threatened with eviction – is liable to be put off seeing a solicitor by fear of the cost, and by not knowing the form. In court cases between landlords and tenants, most landlords have lawyers representing them; tenants rarely do.

The 700 Citizens' Advice Bureaux (CABx) in England, Wales and Northern Ireland, with their 1100 outreach services, are an invaluable filter into the legal system, simply because they tackle all sorts of problems. Therefore, as long as someone recognizes he has a problem, he need not diagnose it himself as a legal one. The advice worker analyses the problem and refers it to the appropriate place for treatment. Advice workers can deal with some of the queries: explaining legislation, filling in forms, making telephone calls, drafting letters or referring the inquirer to a specialist agency. A few CABx have their own salaried lawyers on tap, but most bureaux refer their more difficult legal queries to local solicitors with contracts to provide help as part of the Community Legal Service (see p. 198). A similar role is played by the more diverse group of 850 community-based independent advice agencies affiliated to the Federation of Independent Advice Centres. Most offer general advice on money, housing, welfare benefits and racial discrimination, while others target specific problems such as debt, or particular groups – Bengali women, for instance. A few CABx and other agencies provide representation before employment tribunals and social security appeal tribunals.

Bringing the solicitor to the client can help overcome the reluctance felt by many people to enter the unfamiliar territory of a solicitor's office. About two-thirds of the CABx in England and Wales have visiting lawyers in attendance, usually once a week. Consultations are free. Many areas have local referral schemes, under which solicitors offer clients referred by CABx or advice agencies a free initial half-hour interview. The interview is intended to explore whether the client's problem has a legal remedy and, if so, what steps could be taken to remedy it.

But many people who could be helped by the law are unaware of the services offered by CABx and other agencies. Others go unhelped simply because it never occurs to them that any help might be available to them. Accident victims are an obvious example.

Not every accident victim has a legal remedy. Some accidents are nobody's fault. But the law does allow anyone injured by someone else's negligence to claim compensation for financial loss, as well as pain and suffering. Most serious accidents are someone else's fault – usually traffic accidents and accidents at work. The fact that the victim may be partly responsible – by not wearing a seat-belt, or protective clothing at work – does not bar a compensation claim. It simply reduces the amount of money that the victim will receive. Studies have shown that many accident victims, even with quite serious injuries, don't realize they can claim compensation. A 1984 study by the Centre for Socio-Legal Studies at Oxford found that only one in four of those with serious injuries even thought about claiming damages. Since then, however, accident victims seem to have grown more aware of their right to claim compensation. *Paths to Justice*, a large survey by Hazel Genn of University College London and the National Centre for Social Research, published in 1999, found that about seven out of 10 respondents who suffered accidents or work-related health problems sought advice. One scheme likely to have played a part in raising awareness is the Law Society's Accident Legal Advice Service (ALAS), which could serve as a blueprint for other areas of the law. Launched in June 1986, ALAS covered the whole of England and Wales. The scheme had three aims:

1 to make accident victims realize they might have a claim;
2 to overcome their uncertainty about how to approach a solicitor; and
3 to allay their fears about possible costs.

Leaflets and posters with a helpline number went out to hospitals, doctors' surgeries, CABx, Department of Social Security offices and advice agencies, offering a free interview with a solicitor. In 1994 the scheme was relaunched as Accident Line, with cases referred only to solicitors belonging to the Law Society's panel of personal injury specialists, ensuring that claims are handled by solicitors competent to deal with them.

Publicity, available at the point where those who need it are likely to see it, is the most effective way of getting over the first big hurdle blocking access to the legal system – the lack of awareness of what the system has to offer. The *Paths to Justice* survey interviewed more than 1100 people who, in the previous five years, had experienced one or more 'non-trivial' problems with a possible legal solution. This showed that, while a high proportion of people sought advice for some categories of problem (82 per cent for divorce and separation, for example), those experiencing some other types of problem were much less likely to seek outside help. Only eight per cent, for example, of those with money problems, 13 per cent with landlord problems, and 25 per cent with neighbour problems sought advice. One in five who took no advice felt nothing could be done about the problem. Others thought it would be too much trouble or too expensive.

There is a large information gap in people's awareness of their legal rights. The *Paths to Justice* survey revealed widespread ignorance about the legal system. Such legal knowledge as people had came largely from newspapers and television. The new Community Legal Service (CLS) (which, from April 2000, has replaced the civil legal aid scheme) aims to provide legal information as well as advice and representation. The intention is to help people avoid disputes as well as assisting those embroiled in disputes to resolve them. The internet is seen as a key tool for delivering information and advice, eventually via home television sets. A key plank of the CLS is its *Just Ask!* website, which will search for the answer to a query across 400 legal information websites (www.justask.org.uk). The National Association of Citizens' Advice Bureaux (NACAB) has an advice website (launched in 1999) and many bureaux will give advice by e-mail. This could help to relieve the pressures which greater job insecurity, family breakdown, and the increasingly tenuous lifeline provided by the welfare state are creating for CABx, where callers are likely to be met by engaged tones and long waits for advice. An important aim of the CLS is to link up the services which, at present, are poorly co-ordinated, so that advice seekers, whatever portal they enter, will be directed to the appropriate place for help. It remains to be seen whether the CLS will be able to deliver on its ambitious hopes. It will have a big knowledge gap and a big pool of unmet need to fill.

## Cost

Fear of the cost is the second deterrent to seeking legal help. Newspapers regularly carry frightening stories about losers in legal actions who face bills of tens of thousands of pounds. These scare stories put off even those in the lowest income group, whose legal costs, if their cases are deemed sufficiently meritorious, may well be met by the state. The Community Legal Service, the successor to civil legal aid, pays private practice lawyers and not-for-profit agencies such as law centres and CABx for looking after the legal needs of the less well-off. One big category of case, personal injury – compensation claims by accident victims – are now excluded from state funding, except for very high cost cases. Instead, lawyers handle accident cases on a no-win, no-fee basis, charging no fees unless they win the case (*see* Chapter IX).

Ignorance about the scope and even the existence of state funding for legal help is widespread. In a 1990 Gallup poll, only 45 per cent of people who were asked whether they knew of a scheme providing help with solicitors' charges mentioned legal aid and seven out of ten did not understand how the scheme worked.

State funded legal help is discussed in detail in Chapter IX. It is touched on here because access to justice hinges on access to free or affordable help. The legal aid scheme was set up in 1950 as part of the welfare state with the aim of putting the law and its remedies within the reach of people of 'small or moderate means'. But over the years the middle income group has been squeezed out of the state scheme. This leaves a large chunk of the population outside the scheme yet unable to afford to pay lawyers themselves. In a 1998 policy paper on the proposed new CLS, the Consumers' Association said:

Twenty years ago obtaining legal advice was relatively simple. Most people in the workforce were trades union members, and if they had a problem about work they went to their union. For shopping problems, many major shopping centres had a consumer advice centre; otherwise they could call into their local CAB for some quick help. When all else failed, most people were eligible for legal aid. Now only a minority of people belong to unions; the consumer advice centre has closed; the CAB's waiting room is full to bursting; and most people cannot afford a solicitor.

England's court-based adversarial legal system – with its reliance on expensive lawyers putting the case for each side, its dependence on oral argument and its cumbersome and long-winded procedures – prices justice out of the reach of most individuals. Hence the inexorable rise in the legal aid budget, as more people became aware of their rights and sought to enforce them. Reforms to the machinery of litigation, introduced in 1999, aim to make the process quicker, simpler and cheaper, particularly for smaller cases. Claims of up to £5000 are dealt with by informal arbitration (*see* pp. 12–13); up to £15,000, cases are allocated to a fast track, with strict timetables, limited time in court and fixed costs for lawyers. Throughout the system, judges exercise control over costs to try to ensure they stay in proportion to the claim. (*See* Chapter VII for more detail on these reforms.) But the system is still too expensive for most people to fund their own litigation.

Many decisions which affect the lives of ordinary people are not made by courts, but by tribunals. Employment tribunals decide whether someone has been unfairly dismissed, and claimants refused welfare benefits can appeal to a social security appeals tribunal. But for most tribunals, free representation is available to only a limited extent, although studies show that representation significantly increases the chances of success.

Criminal charges are covered by legal aid. In the Crown Court, where the more serious charges are tried, legal aid is freely given. Almost all defendants have their defences paid for by the state. Legal aid is usually granted as long as the financial test is satisfied – broadly, if the defendant needs help in meeting the cost of his defence – which it almost always is, since few defendants can afford to finance the costs of a Crown Court trial out of their own pockets.

In the magistrates' court, however, where the less serious criminal cases (95 per cent) are disposed of, legal aid is more discretionary. Some courts are more liberal than others. Yet the cost of employing a lawyer means that for most defendants no legal aid means no lawyer and, therefore, less chance of a favourable outcome.

## Duty solicitors and advisers

One development of the 1970s which has improved access to justice in the magistrates' court is the duty solicitor scheme. Duty solicitors, paid for by the state without a means test, are on call day and night to advise defendants brought before the court on criminal charges. Should a defendant plead guilty or is there a legal defence worth pursuing? The solicitor can apply for bail and ask for an adjournment to allow time to apply for legal aid and prepare the case. If the defendant pleads guilty, the duty solicitor can make a 'plea in mitigation', putting forward reasons which might influence the magistrates to impose a lighter sentence than they might otherwise.

Suspects have the right of access to legal advice in the police station, and around 40 per cent take advantage of that right. For those who don't have their own solicitors, duty solicitors provide advice on a 24 hour basis at police stations. Advice, which is free to the suspect, is paid for by the state.

In around thirty county courts, CAB workers act as duty advisers, mostly for small debtors and tenants faced with eviction by local councils and private landlords. The government hopes to make such help more widely available as part of the Community Legal Service.

## Finding the right solicitor

How does someone with a legal problem find the right solicitor to handle it? Traditionally, the system was fairly hit and miss, but recent developments are making it easier. Several studies have investigated how people find a solicitor. In one study involving divorcing parents, by far the most popular method of choosing was through the recommendation of family or friends. The next largest group went to a solicitor they had used before – in many cases for their house purchase. Nearly one person in six had simply noticed a solicitor's office and walked in, or chosen a firm from the *Yellow Pages*. Only about one in eight asked the CAB or a social worker, though in most areas the CAB will be the agency with most experience of local solicitors and their work.

In a survey carried out for the Law Society in 1986, 60 per cent of people found a solicitor through recommendation by friends, relatives, work colleagues, banks, estate agents or other professionals. Around 26 per cent used the solicitor they always used, or the family solicitor. Later Law Society surveys have produced similar results: in a 1989 survey 43 per cent selected a solicitor through recommendations from friends, relatives, banks, building societies or estate agents, while seven per cent chose a firm because its office was conveniently located. Another 28 per cent had a solicitor they always used or a family solicitor. In a 1994 survey, the most common reason for choosing a particular solicitor was having used that solicitor before, followed by recommendation. A 1999 study of people who used solicitors' services on a no-win, no-fee basis found that many of them chose their solicitor through advertising, and a convenient location was an important factor.

In 1985 the Law Society relaxed its rules to allow solicitors to advertise the type of work they do and the fees they charge, but not to claim any expertise or specialization. Since 1990 solicitors have been allowed to advertise themselves as specialists, but they are not allowed to make such a claim unless it can be justified.

A growing move towards accreditation of specialist solicitors is making it easier to match the right solicitor to the case. The Law Society accredits solicitors to specialist panels in several categories of work: child care law, mental health law, planning law, personal injury, clinical negligence, family law and immigration. A criminal law panel is expected to be launched in July 2000, with housing law and family mediation panels to follow. The charity Action for Victims of Medical

Accidents (AVMA) also maintains a panel of solicitors who specialize in clinical negligence.

Legal aid franchising, introduced in 1993, helped the public to identify solicitors reaching minimum levels of experience and competence. Solicitors' firms meeting certain standards were granted franchises in particular fields of work – for example, family law or crime – entitling them to more favourable terms, including quicker payments. The fact that a firm has a franchise indicates at least that it does a reasonable volume of work in the field and meets criteria set by the Commission for efficiency and case management. State-funded clinical negligence, family and immigration cases may be handled only by firms with a franchise for that work, to ensure that the taxpayer is buying expertise. The franchise also operates as a guarantee of a firm's specialization for clients who don't qualify for state funding. As of January 2000, state-funded advice and help short of court proceedings is available only through law firms, law centres and advice agencies with a contract to provide the help. By April 2001 all state-funded work will be carried out under contracts, which will be granted only to those with proven expertise and experience.

## Other sources of help

For many people the prospect of visiting a solicitor's office can be rather forbidding. Law centres, with their shop-front offices and casually dressed staff, seem more approachable. For those fortunate enough to receive it, law centre help is usually of quite a high standard. The trouble is that law centres are thin on the ground: there are only about 50 in England and Wales. Run by salaried lawyers and advice workers, these offer a free legal service to the poorer section of the community within their catchment area, although there is no formal means test. So as not to compete with solicitors in private practice, they are not allowed to do certain types of work – divorce, conveyancing and large personal injury cases, for example – and they tend to concentrate on housing, immigration, employment, and welfare benefits. Law centres have good contacts with private solicitors in their area, particularly those who do law centre-type work, and will refer clients to outside solicitors if they cannot take on a job themselves. Some law centres prefer to spread their resources by concentrating on groups, rather than individuals – for example, tackling a local authority over disrepair on a whole council estate.

In some areas legal advice centres – run by local authorities, church groups, residents' associations or other agencies – offer free advice but (unlike law centres) won't usually take on cases and see them through. These centres usually have no legally qualified staff of their own, but depend on volunteer lawyers who are willing to give up some of their spare time.

Most trades unions offer legal help and advice to their members. Some offer general advice while others restrict themselves to legal problems connected with the member's job – such as accidents at work, sacking, breaches of the employment contract. Some unions have their own legal departments which handle negotiations in accident cases, and represent union members at employment tribunals. Unions also retain solicitors in private practice to deal with accident claims on behalf of their members.

Many other organizations provide legal help or simple advice to members or to the general public, on either a commercial or a voluntary basis. The Automobile Association, for example, has its own legal staff which deals with members' motoring-related legal problems, as the Consumers' Association does for consumer problems. Some voluntary agencies, such as MIND (The National Association for Mental Health), will advise, take up cases and provide representation before tribunals. Some local authorities run housing and consumer advice centres, and government-funded bodies such as the Equal Opportunities Commission and the Commission for Racial Equality will answer legal queries in their own fields and help with tribunals and court cases.

The Bar's Free Representation Unit (FRU) provides representation mainly by Bar students and young barristers at tribunals and Criminal Injuries Compensation Authority hearings. Cases are taken only on referral, chiefly from CABx in Greater London.

The Bar and the solicitors' branch of the profession have each set up *pro bono* groups – the Latin tag (short for *pro bono publico*: for the public good) lawyers use to describe the unpaid legal work they do. The Bar Pro Bono Unit co-ordinates a panel of barristers, including QCs, who volunteer to work free of charge for at least three days a year; some take on cases which last much longer. Cases, which cover a wide range of subject matter, come from 'litigants in person' (people representing themselves – *see* below), solicitors, CABx, law centres and advice agencies. The unit has a panel of solicitors with whom its barristers work as a *pro bono* team. The Solicitors Pro Bono Group provides advice and support for solicitors' firms in setting up *pro bono* projects and co-ordinating their unpaid work. It plans in future to refer cases from law centres, community groups and charities to solicitors who do *pro bono* work.

## Do-it-yourself law

Given the gaps in legal aid and the cost of legal services (which we explore in more detail in Chapter IX), what scope is there for taking the law into your own hands?

The United Kingdom is a nation of do-it-yourselfers. If you can do your own gardening, car maintenance and decorating, why not a DIY will, conveyance or divorce? Will-making is superficially simple, and home-made wills are common, but many of them turn out to be invalid, usually because of the simplest mistakes, like failing to sign the will or have it properly witnessed. DIY conveyancing is still fairly uncommon because the legal procedure for buying and selling houses is complicated and time-consuming, and full of unfamiliar terminology or language. Conveyancing charges are not high, and most people are unwilling to take a chance that something might go wrong when buying an asset in which much of their wealth is tied up. But step-by-step manuals are available for DIY lawyers who are prepared to tackle conveyancing, will-making, divorce-by-post, and the work involved in sorting out an estate.

A growing number of people, unable to afford lawyers, are taking their own cases to court, though this is not an easy task. Despite changes to the civil justice system in 1999 to make it easier and cheaper, the system is very much designed for lawyers. So litigants in person find themselves at a substantial disadvantage. In 1997, a study of county courts (which deal with the smaller civil claims) by John Baldwin of the Institute of Judicial Administration at Birmingham University discovered that litigants in person found court hearings daunting and fewer than half felt they had coped well. At the Royal Courts of Justice in London, which houses the Court of Appeal and the main centre for the High Court, a citizens' advice bureau (with volunteer lawyers on a rota) helps litigants in person with their cases, but the bureau is hard-pressed to cope with the demand. Litigants in person are usually allowed to have a friend in court – known as a 'McKenzie friend' from the leading case in which the right was upheld – to prompt, advise and help, but not to speak on their behalf. The Court of Appeal decided, in 1999, that the right to have a Mckenzie friend was not an absolute right, but that it should normally be allowed unless the judge decided that 'fairness and the interests of justice' did not require it in a particular case.

## Small claims

Since 1973 a small claims procedure has operated within the county courts. District judges – the lowest tier of the full-time judiciary – act as arbitrators. Lawyers are not banned but, in most cases, the loser won't be ordered to pay the winner's costs. So litigants risk only the court fees if they lose plus, possibly, a small amount for the other side's loss of earnings and expenses while attending the hearing, and a maximum of £200 towards an expert's fees.

Under reforms to the civil justice system in 1999, claims of £5000 or less will normally be allocated to the small claims track. (For personal injury and housing disrepair cases the limit is £1000.) The judge may give permission for an expert to be hired to make a report and possibly give evidence at the hearing, if this is necessary to prove the case. Agreeing with the other side to use the same expert can save costs. If the case is too complicated to be dealt with as a small claim, the judge will allocate it to the 'fast-track' (a streamlined procedure for claims up to £15,000, with hearings in open court).

In the small claims track, the parties to the dispute sit around a table in the district judge's room, rather than in a formal courtroom. Typical disputes, normally resolved in a hearing of an hour or so, are over faulty consumer goods, debts, holidays, building work or car repairs which failed to come up to expectation. Small claims deliver a rough and ready type of justice, but claimants must still prove their claims according to legal standards. They are likely to need evidence, such as bills or other documents, photographs and experts' reports, and getting advice beforehand will improve the chances of success.

Although the process is meant to be simple and informal, many individuals still find preparing and presenting the case daunting and time-consuming. Just as many businesses as individuals use the procedure and in a number of cases at least one side – usually a company or a shopkeeper – is represented by a lawyer. Non-lawyers, such as friends or consumer advisers, may represent a party at a small claims hearing.

The Birmingham University study in 1997 (see above) found that three out of four litigants who had gone through the small claims process were happy with the way their cases were handled. However, court fees are a deterrent where the sum in dispute is fairly small. And having gone through what is still, for many people, a daunting and protracted procedure and won the case, the successful litigant is all too often let down by the ineffective system for enforcing judgments, which puts the onus entirely on him to pursue his opponent through yet more court procedures. The Birmingham University study found that many claimants had not realized that getting judgment was just the first stage, and many were 'shocked and disillusioned' when they discovered that the defendant had no intention of paying up. 'For many plaintiffs, the court hearing merely marks the end of round one in what might well prove to be a prolonged, acrimonious, and ultimately fruitless contest.' The government is considering ways of making the enforcement system more effective.

# Alternative dispute resolution (ADR)

Alternative dispute resolution (ADR) is an umbrella term for methods of resolving legal disputes without going through formal and costly court proceedings. Arbitration and mediation are the two main types of ADR. The main advantages are informality, cheapness and speed. With arbitration, the two parties agree to be bound by the decision of a third party who arbitrates between them. The small claims procedure is an example, with the district judge acting as arbitrator. Other examples are the trade arbitration schemes used to resolve customer complaints in a number of consumer service industries, such as the travel business.

With mediation, the two parties to the dispute try to reach an agreement themselves, with the third party acting as a go-between or facilitator. Mediation is widely used in divorce, but in some other spheres where it has been tried in place of litigation – medical negligence, for example – the take-up has been low, mainly because of lawyers' reluctance to depart from traditional methods of resolving disputes. Under the 1999 reforms to the civil justice system, judges may allow a temporary halt to a case while the parties try to settle it by mediation or arbitration.

The government is keen on promoting the use of ADR as an alternative to traditional litigation. The Lord Chancellor announced in April 2000 that a pilot mediation scheme would be set up in Leeds, to encourage people to resolve their disputes away from the courtroom.

# CHAPTER II

# The Courts

The courtroom is the pivot of the English system of justice. For centuries it has been the setting for the final settlement of disputes, whether between the state and one of its citizens said to have committed a wrong against society, or between individuals. And because the contest in the court itself can be so crucial, much more than in most other countries (where many of the more important decisions are taken before the trial), the English courtroom has been invested with a sense of high drama and tension. Lives can be ruined and fortunes made there. What God has joined together can, in a court, be put asunder. One judge, three magistrates or 12 ordinary men and women can hold in their hands a person's freedom, reputation, wealth, home, marriage and happiness.

The American journalist H. L. Mencken described a courtroom as a place where Jesus Christ and Judas Iscariot would be equals, with the betting odds in favour of Judas. Books and television programmes have confirmed the courtroom as a place of drama and uncertainty, where justice fights injustice and often lands up on the losing side, and where victory depends on fate, often in the guise of a last-minute surprise witness.

The reality is very different. The activities of an English court are, for the most part, of little interest to anyone other than the parties involved. Far from crackling with electric tension, the atmosphere droops with soporific indifference. Every now and again there is a criminal trial which excites the public interest because of the personality involved, like Lester Piggott or Gary Glitter, or famous figures in the City charged with fraud (Robert Maxwell's sons Kevin and Ian), or because of the sheer magnitude of the crime (Rosemary West, the

Yorkshire Ripper, Dr Harold Shipman). Sometimes, it is the issue raised that excites the public – euthanasia in the case of Dr David Moor, charged with the murder of a terminally ill patient (he was acquitted); 'date rape'; wives who kill their violent husbands after suffering years of abuse and threats and find that there are no legal defences open to them on a charge of murder; or the Official Secrets Act charge against Clive Ponting over the leaking of background information on the Falklands War. But the vast majority of criminal trials are humdrum affairs. Indeed, most defendants plead guilty and all that is done in the courtroom is the sentencing. Whether or not he goes to prison, and for how long, is of course tremendously important to the defendant and to those close to him. But it is not often the stuff of great drama, and much else that happens in court is merely formal or procedural: remands, requests for bail, etc.

The civil courts present an even drier prospect to the outside observer. Here too there is much that is mere conveyor-belt procedure: various kinds of applications and petitions to the court which do not involve a real contest. In trials which are fought out, argument on legal points often takes up a large part of the time, and even the cross-examination of witnesses seldom raises the low-key pitch of the proceedings. Even cases of great public interest, like those over the fate of the former Chilean dictator General Pinochet, and about *Spycatcher*, the book written by a former MI5 officer that the government tried to ban, are conducted in a subdued, almost boring, manner. Libel trials involving celebrities like *Eastenders* star Gillian Taylforth, the Holocaust-denying historian David Irving, the lying MP Jonathan Aitken, or the contest between Mohamed al Fayed and the disgraced MP Neil Hamilton, attract a lot of media coverage and can be entertaining; but by no means are all libel trials that dramatic.

The Court of Appeal, for its part, very rarely hears witnesses at all, and the appeal is based mainly or totally on legal argument, impenetrable to those who are uninitiated in the jargon.

The visual image that most people have of an English court is becoming increasingly wrong, too. Those elegant, high-ceilinged, wood-panelled rooms, with the judge viewing proceedings from his vantage point behind a resplendent oak table on a raised platform, are dying out. The new courts are small, functional, low-ceilinged and often lit with artificial fluorescent lighting. The judge's pedestal has shrunk and he is lower and nearer everyone else in the courtroom. The effect is bland, clinical and cheerless.

## The structure of the courts

Like so many other English legal institutions, the court system defies logical analysis. It is the product of 900 years of development, much of it haphazard and unplanned, punctuated by occasional attempts by Parliament to bring some order into it and adapt it to changing needs. There is certainly a recognizable hierarchy, with the House of Lords as the 'highest court in the land' (though its supremacy is no longer absolute, since membership of the European Union makes our laws subject to the European Court of Justice in Luxembourg). But it is not a straightforward, clearly mapped out pyramid structure, as in most other countries. There are deviations and quirks and historical accidents clouding the symmetry. Probably the most logical dividing line is between the criminal and the civil courts, though in fact some courts do both kinds of work.

What is the difference between civil and criminal cases? In a criminal case someone is prosecuted for conduct, which we call criminal, which is considered harmful to society as a whole. There are, of course, individual victims of murder or burglary but, in a wider sense, all crimes affect us all. So, normally the prosecution is brought by the state (using the Queen's name – cases are listed as Regina v. Accused), although individuals may also bring a prosecution. If found guilty, the offender will be punished by the state.

Civil cases are between private interests. An individual (or company, local authority or some other organization) sues another, usually for some harm caused to him personally, or for money owed to him. Perhaps the person he is suing has run him down and fractured his leg, or has broken a contract. The police will not be interested unless the same behaviour also amounts to a crime. For example, a driver who knocks down a pedestrian may be guilty of the crime of dangerous or careless driving. The same accident gives the victim the right to sue the driver for the tort (legal terminology for a civil wrong) of negligence. So the driver can be prosecuted for dangerous driving in a criminal court, convicted and sent to prison or ordered to pay a fine, which goes to the state. Later he may be sued by the person he has injured, found negligent, and be ordered to pay compensation to the victim for the injury suffered. Or he may win one case and lose the other, because different things have to be proved in civil and criminal cases. The degree of proof required is also different. In criminal cases there can only be a conviction if the case has been proved 'beyond reasonable doubt' – very near certainty. A civil case is won on the less difficult test of 'balance of probabilities' – is it more likely than not?

In civil cases, the person suing was, until 1999, known as the plaintiff, but is now officially called the claimant, and the person sued is the defendant. In criminal cases, the person accused of the crime is called either the accused or the defendant.

The distinction between a crime and a civil wrong was highlighted in 1982 when an intruder broke into the Queen's bedroom at Buckingham Palace. Entering someone else's home without permission is trespass: not a crime, but a civil wrong. It only becomes a crime if the intruder uses, or threatens to use, violence, or causes damage, say by breaking a lock or a window, or if he intends to commit a crime (such as theft) once inside. Because Michael Fagan's intrusion was a simple trespass, he could not be prosecuted for that, although the incident did lead to (unsuccessful) calls for that kind of trespass to be made a crime. But a trespasser can be sued in the civil courts. (It follows that the sign 'Trespassers will be prosecuted' doesn't make sense, legally.)

New crimes are being created all the time, as society revises its thinking about the sorts of behaviour it wants to discourage. For example, insider dealing in the City only became a crime in the mid-1980s, even though the practice had been going on for many years. New technology can result in new crimes – computer hacking, for example, has been made a criminal offence.

It is a fundamental principle of English justice that what happens in the courts should be open and public. There are exceptions, such as where young children are involved, or there is a risk to national security. But, in general, English justice is open justice, and any member of the public can see what goes on in any court.

This section gives an outline of the structure and jurisdiction of the courts themselves: the judges, magistrates and other personnel of the courts are discussed more fully in Chapters III and V.

## Magistrates' courts

Magistrates' courts are the people's courts (once popularly known as police courts) and are the lowest tier in the criminal justice system. They have been with us in one form or another for 600 years, and magistrates (justices of the peace, or JPs) for even longer. Originally a sort of primitive policing agency, JPs were given their judicial role in the fourteenth century. The magistrates and their courts have undergone a number of changes in their status, jurisdiction and reputation since then but the fundamental basis of their existence has remained the same. Justice is delivered not by professional judges or lawyers, but by appointed representatives of the community.

The system of unpaid, largely untrained, volunteer, part-time magistrates is unique in the world. There are more than 30,000 lay magistrates, plus around 100 paid, legally qualified magistrates (known as stipendiaries, but their new official title is district judge (magistrates courts)). They sit in more than 400 courts in England and Wales (the system is different in Scotland and Northern Ireland), and deal with around two million criminal cases a year, more than 95 per cent of all criminal proceedings, as well as performing a variety of other functions.

Their main job is to deliver 'summary justice' to people charged with less serious crimes. (Grave offences are dealt with at the Crown Court.) But the fact that they deal with the lower end of the criminal market does not mean that the punishments they impose are necessarily trivial. For some offences magistrates can send offenders to prison for six months. Some 48,000 adults were jailed by magistrates in 1998, and 4500 youths (under 18s) were placed in custody.

Most defendants who come before the magistrates' courts plead guilty to the charges against them and all the magistrates do is pass sentence on them or, occasionally, send them to the Crown Court for a more severe punishment than the magistrates have the power to impose. For those who plead not guilty to some offences, there has up to now been a choice between having their trial by magistrates but no jury, or going to the Crown Court for a jury trial. Such 'either-way' offences include less serious assaults and burglaries, theft, and dangerous driving. For trivial offences, however, there is no choice – the law lays down that the charge must be heard by the magistrates.

A highly controversial Bill going through Parliament at the time of writing is aimed at eliminating an accused's right to choose trial by jury for the middle-ranking 'either-way' offences. Instead, the decision would be taken by the magistrates themselves. The accused would have the opportunity to put his case for having a jury trial, and would have the right of appeal to a Crown Court judge if it were refused, but critics (including many who normally support the government) see the proposed law as an attack on the citizen's traditional fundamental rights which would result in more innocent people being convicted. For its part, the government's intention is to save the time and money involved in thousands of defendants choosing jury trial and then, sometimes at the last minute, pleading guilty anyway (see also Chapter VI).

Trial and sentencing are not the only functions of magistrates' courts in the criminal justice system. Magistrates make crucial decisions over whether to grant a defendant bail or to remand him to prison to wait for his trial.

They act, too, as filters through which many serious criminal cases pass on their way to the Crown Court. Under these 'committal proceedings' the magistrates look at the documents in a case to make sure that there is enough evidence against an accused to warrant a Crown Court trial. Committal proceedings once used to be a genuine inquiry into the strength of the evidence, sometimes with witnesses giving evidence before the magistrates, but nowadays they are usually little more than a rubber-stamping exercise. The aim is to get rid of them altogether and let the Crown Prosecution Service decide whether there is enough evidence.

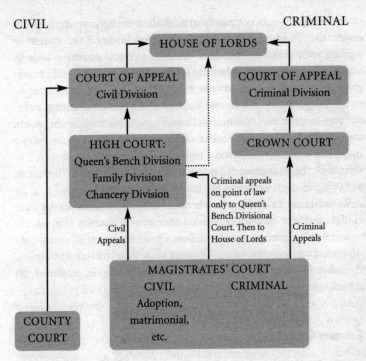

CIVIL                                    CRIMINAL

*Simplified diagram of English courts*

Children under 18 accused of criminal offences are usually dealt with in youth courts. They are supposed to be more informal and less frightening than the adult courts, and separate from them. Youth courts stress the care and treatment of young delinquents, rather than their punishment. Because they deal with such sensitive matters, the public is excluded from these courts. The magistrates who sit in youth courts are specially selected from the pool of all JPs for their knowledge of and interest in children. The Labour Home Secretary, Jack Straw, made the speeding up of youth justice a priority, so that guilty young offenders can be dealt with as soon as possible after the crime, and not many months later.

In the non-criminal part of their work, specially chosen magistrates sit in the family proceedings courts, dealing with many applications under the Children Act 1989, which revolutionized the system of dealing with children at risk of abuse or neglect, or whose parents cannot cope with them. Magistrates have powers to deal with emergencies and to make various other orders affecting children.

The magistrates' courts are also responsible for granting drink licences to pubs and restaurants, and licences for betting shops and casinos. It is a duty which JPs take seriously. They are no rubber stamp, as the Ladbroke and Playboy casino empires discovered to their cost; their activities came to a stop as a direct result of the refusal of five licensing magistrates to renew their licences.

Requests for extradition – where a foreign state asks for an individual wanted by them to be handed over for that country to prosecute – are usually heard at London's Bow Street magistrates' court, by a stipendiary magistrate. Spain's request to Britain to extradite General Pinochet to face trial in Spain was a sensational example of the extradition process.

## Crown Courts

Crown Courts have existed only since 1972, when they replaced the ancient quarter sessions and assize courts. They are the places where all the serious crimes are tried, such as murder, rape, arson, armed robbery, fraud and so on, as well as some less serious offences. Until 2000, even the most trivial theft, involving only a few pence, could be dealt with in the Crown Court if the accused wanted it. But, under a proposed new law (see p. 20), that automatic right to choose would be taken away from an accused, and it would be for the magistrates to decide whether or not to send a case to the Crown Court for trial by jury. That would mean many thousands fewer cases reaching the Crown Court.

When there is a jury, the judge's role is limited to deciding matters of law, and summing-up to the jury. The jury decides whether the defendant is guilty or not guilty. But of the more than 95,000 defendants dealt with by the Crown Court in 1998, only about 30,000 eventually had a trial by jury, of whom nearly 65 per cent were acquitted. The others had either pleaded guilty originally, or had changed their plea from not guilty to guilty (sometimes at the last minute, even on the day of trial) and needed only to be sentenced.

There are 90 Crown Court centres in England and Wales, many of them consisting of several courtrooms. According to the seriousness of the charges, cases can be tried by High Court judges (the most important crimes – murder, for instance – or particularly sensitive cases), circuit judges (who hear the majority of Crown Court trials), or part-time recorders.

The most famous Crown Court in England, perhaps the most famous court in the world, is the Old Bailey, or more properly, the Central Criminal Court. Built on the site of the notorious Newgate Prison, the Old Bailey has been host to some of the most famous and infamous murderers in English history, among them Dr Crippen, Christie, the Yorkshire Ripper, the Kray twins, and Ruth Ellis (the last woman to be hanged for murder in England). For many of them it was their last public appearance before the gallows. Oscar Wilde and William Joyce (wartime's Lord Haw-Haw, executed for high treason) were among other participants in the court's dramatic history.

The death penalty has now been abolished; crowds seldom queue for hours to get into an Old Bailey court as they used to. And the great barristers of the court's golden era, Edward Marshall Hall, Patrick Hastings and Norman Birkett, have been replaced by humdrum, less flamboyant, less eccentric barristers, boring perhaps but effective. Most of the Old Bailey's 18 courtrooms are now in a new uninspiring annexe, lacking all atmosphere. However, the figure on the dome of the Old Bailey building of the lady holding the scales of justice (and, contrary to public belief, not blindfolded) remains one of the enduring symbols of justice in a free society.

The Crown Court acts also as the appeal court against both convictions and sentences by magistrates. When the appeal is against conviction, the Crown Court judge rehears all the evidence that witnesses have already given in the lower court, but there is no jury. For all appeals the judge sits with lay magistrates, usually two of them.

## County courts

Just as the magistrates' courts deal with the vast majority of those criminal cases at the less serious end of the scale, county courts take on most of the smaller civil cases. Partly it is the amount of money involved that determines whether the county court will be entitled to try a civil claim, but the complexity or legal importance of a case is also a factor. Difficult cases will go to the High Court, as will claims involving very large sums of money. In general (and there are a lot of exceptions) county courts will deal with claims involving less than £50,000. The courts deal with more than two million cases a year, the vast majority of them money claims – payment for goods sold, or fees for work done. They also hear personal injury claims, repossession actions by building societies against mortgage defaulters, disputes between landlord and tenant (mostly actions by landlords to get their property back), cases involving wills and estates, and the winding up of companies. Some courts also deal with bankruptcies.

Small claims, up to £5000, are dealt with by a special procedure, designed to be quicker, cheaper and more informal than the normal (*see* Chapter I). County courts also have jurisdiction over most matrimonial matters. They can grant divorces and make a range of orders relating to money, property and children; they have the power to order a violent husband or lover out of the home.

There are county courts all over England and Wales, around 220 altogether. The judges have the rank of circuit judge, the same level as those who sit in the Crown Court. There are also more junior judges, known as district judges (formerly registrars), who decide county court divorce disputes over property and money, arbitrate in small claims and deal with pre-trial procedural issues.

## The High Court

The High Court is a hotch-potch. It is a composite entity embracing three separate kinds of court – called divisions – each with separate functions (although they occasionally overlap) and descending from an even greater confusion of ancient courts, going back to the twelfth century. The 102 High Court judges are distributed between the three divisions, which have their home in London's Royal Courts of Justice, an eccentric Victorian Neo-Gothic building on the Strand, with sittings in some provincial towns and cities.

The biggest of the divisions, with 69 judges and the widest jurisdiction, is the Queen's Bench (King's Bench when the reigning monarch is male). Its most important function is as the main civil court for disputes that are too complex or important for the county court to deal with, or that involve large sums of money. Claims for money owing are the High Court's main staple, with actions for damages arising from motor and work accidents, and breach of contract cases, the next most popular. It also deals with libel suits, which, though relatively few in number, frequently get a lot of publicity because of the personalities involved. The division also includes a commercial court, which specializes in large commercial disputes, an admiralty court for shipping cases and a technology and construction court dealing with large building disputes.

The Divisional Court of the Queen's Bench Division (one, two or three judges sitting, depending on the type of case) provides one of the most important safeguards of a citizen's fundamental right to liberty in our society. The court can issue the famous and ancient writ of *habeas corpus* (literally, 'you shall have the body'), ordering the release of an individual who has been unlawfully detained, for instance by the police or by immigration authorities.

The Divisional Court's role as protector against abuse of power goes further. It is the main court of review for administrative decisions taken by bodies vested with some legal authority, such as government departments and local authorities. Challenges to such executive power are made under a procedure known as 'judicial review', which, following some well-publicized cases, has become an increasingly popular way of trying to contest controversial government and local council policies, when the decision-makers in question have exceeded their legal powers or acted unreasonably. That part of the Queen's Bench Division which deals with such public and administrative law cases will in future be known as the Administrative Court, its judges specialists in those fields of law.

The range of subjects which have come before the court on judicial review – some 4500 cases in 1998 – is extremely wide; it includes immigration, housing, environment, schooling, planning, transport and prisons. Judicial review has been used – successfully – to make the Home Secretary think again about granting a pardon to the executed Derek Bentley, to rule that the Foreign Secretary was not entitled to use certain public funds for the building of a dam in Malaysia, and to decide that the government's licensing of oil and gas exploration did not take enough account of the whales and dolphins in the area.

Unsuccessful attempts to use judicial review include trying to force the Jockey Club to reverse the disqualification of a horse that had won a classic race, and attempting to nullify the government's handling of Britain's accession to the European Union's Maastricht Treaty.

The judges have shown that they are not frightened to find ministerial decisions unlawful. At one stage the government became so worried at the number of cases in which the courts were ruling against ministers that they issued a booklet to civil servants called *The judge over your shoulder*, explaining how to make sure decisions were not overturned by the courts.

The court can also quash decisions of magistrates' courts where they exceed their powers, or there are irregularities in the proceedings, or they get the law wrong. The court does not hear witnesses or deal with cases which raise only factual points.

The Family Division of the High Court has 16 judges plus its head, the President, currently Dame Elizabeth Butler-Sloss, the most senior woman in the judicial hierarchy. The 'bleeding hearts' part of our judicial system, it deals with divorce; disputes between warring spouses involving children, property or money; adoption, wardship and other questions affecting children. Issues of law relating to medical advances come to the court, like Diane Blood's request to be impregnated with her dead husband's sperm. It also makes decisions about the future of people who cannot take decisions themselves, like Tony Bland, the young man in a persistent vegetative state following the

Hillsborough disaster, who was eventually allowed to die with the court's consent. Its judges belie the reputation of the judiciary for being behind the times, conservative and moralistic: they are often in the vanguard of progressive thinking on family matters.

The Chancery Division's 17 judges, plus its head, the Vice-Chancellor, deal with arid (to the outsider) but important areas of law such as tax, interpretation of wills, companies, settlements, trusts and various other issues affecting finance and property. It was the forerunner of the Chancery Division that fell victim to Charles Dickens' vitriolic pen in *Bleak House*:

This is the Court of Chancery; which has its decaying houses and its blighted lands in every shire; which has its worn-out lunatic in every madhouse, and its dead in every churchyard; which has its ruined suitor, with his slipshod heels and threadbare dress, borrowing and begging through the round of every man's acquaintance; which gives to monied might the means abundantly of wearing out the right; which so exhausts finances, patience, courage, hope; so overthrows the brain and breaks the heart; that there is not an honourable man among its practitioners who would not give – who does not often give – the warning, 'Suffer any wrong that can be done you, rather than come here!'

Things have changed a lot since then. The Chancery Division handles cases affecting huge sums of money and nationally important legal financial issues such as, for instance, the fall-out from the Robert Maxwell affair or the Lloyd's insurance crisis. And far from being the most sluggish of courts, the Chancery Division has become one of the most speedy, efficient and dependable.

## The Court of Appeal

The English legal system is in the fortunate, though perhaps unnecessary, position of having a two-tier system of appeals. The Court of Appeal is the main repository of dissatisfaction with the decisions of lower courts. Above it is the House of Lords.

In the Court of Appeal sit the judges who influence and form the law of England, perhaps even more than their superiors in the House of Lords. There are two divisions of the appeal court: the head of the Criminal Division is the Lord Chief Justice, currently Lord Woolf, the country's top professional judge. The Civil Division is led by the Master of the Rolls, soon to be Lord Phillips. It is yet another oddity of the system that these, the two most senior judges, do not sit in the most senior court, the House of Lords. The 35 appeal judges, more formally Lords Justices of Appeal, are at the centre of the law's development. When a written law is uncertain or leaves a gap, it has to be interpreted, and it is the three judges (sometimes two) who sit on each appeal who set most of the precedents that have to be followed by the lower courts, and often make the newspaper headlines.

The Civil Division heard about 1200 appeals in 1998, from the High Court as well as from county courts and a few more specialized courts. The Criminal Division, manned by High Court as well as appeal judges, dealt with nearly 3000 appeals, though most of them were against the sentence only, not the conviction.

The Court of Appeal does not hear witnesses, other than in exceptional circumstances. The decisions are based on documents and transcripts, supplemented by the arguments of barristers, or sometimes of individuals who appear in person.

## The House of Lords

Even the name confuses. The House of Lords is, of course, Parliament's second chamber, made up of peers of the realm. But the term is also used as shorthand to describe those legal members of the House who hear appeals. Law lords, or, to give their formal title, Lords of Appeal in Ordinary, are eminent judges from English, as well as Scottish and Northern Irish, courts. (The House of Lords is the final arbiter not only of all cases from England and Northern Ireland, but also of Scottish civil, though not criminal, cases.) Constitutionally, the appeal is actually to the whole House of Lords and until the nineteenth century non-lawyer peers could and did sit, however much they lacked judicial ability. Only in 1876 was it provided that the job should be given over to experienced judges. But some remnants of the past remain. The law lords do not deliver judgments like all other judges, they make speeches. They do not come to a decision, they take a vote on a motion that the appeal be dismissed or allowed.

There are 12 law lords, of whom two, as is customary, come from the Scottish judiciary and one from Northern Ireland. The Lord Chancellor and former Lord Chancellors are also entitled to sit, and sometimes do. The law lords almost always sit in panels of five (though for very important cases, like General Pinochet's, there can be seven of them), usually in committee rooms in the Houses of Parliament at Westminster. The judges, usually in their sixties, wear ordinary dark suits, with no gowns or wigs, and they sit in a semicircle behind a horseshoe table, not a raised dais or high platform. The discussion on fine points of law, between the barristers and the law lords, is carried out in low voices without histrionics.

There is no automatic right to take an appeal to the House of Lords; permission to do so has to be given either by the Court of Appeal from whose decision the appeal is made, or by the House of Lords itself. The law lords can also hear appeals on criminal issues directly from the Divisional Court, without first going through the Court of Appeal, as they did in General Pinochet's case. In general, law lords will hear only cases involving points of law of public importance. They must have a significance going beyond the individuals involved in the case. In 1999 the law lords decided a mere 60 appeals.

Why is the appeal to the House of Lords necessary? There is already a Court of Appeal manned by some of our best judges, so why another court? It seems an unnecessary luxury to have five appeal judges sitting in judgment on the decision of three scarcely (if at all) less able judges. And it can and does lead to absurd results. Where, for instance, the Court of Appeal has decided three–nil in favour of one side and the House of Lords decides the other way by a margin of three–two, the judgement that becomes the law of the land has the support of only three out of eight of the best judges in the country. The costs of taking a case to one appeal, let alone to two, are prohibitive. There seems to be no logically convincing reason for retaining the double appeal option.

The government's planned reform of the House of Lords has raised a further issue: why should the law lords, the top judges, also be part of the legislature? Should the judiciary not be seen as being totally separate from the parliamentary law-making process? Their membership of the House of Lords is a historical anomaly, not based on logic. The Royal Commission on reforming the upper house, under Lord Wakeham, which reported in 2000, proposed leaving the law lords where they were, but the debate continues, and there is a strong argument for severing the link and creating a separate Supreme Court for our most senior judges, not tied to the legislature.

## Some other courts

The six mainstream courts described above are not by any means an exhaustive list. A number of other, more specialized, courts have been set up to deal with particular areas of the law or to perform special functions.

### The Privy Council

The Judicial Committee of the Privy Council, to give it its full title, is a relic of colonial times. In the days of the British Empire, the Privy Council sat at its centre, London, as the supreme court of appeal for all the colonies and dominions. Britain had provided those countries with a legal system, and it was natural that it should give them the opportunity to come before the most august judges of the motherland. As the Empire waned, so did the Privy Council's influence. Its jurisdiction is now confined to hearing appeals from the remaining colonies, and from those former British territories which have chosen to retain it as their final appeal court. There is something strange about one sovereign country's giving the final right to rule on its laws to the judges of another, and many Commonwealth countries – Canada, India, Australia and most of the African states, for example – have found reference to the Privy Council to be incompatible with their independence. But some – among them New Zealand and a number of Caribbean countries – have chosen to retain it because they think it is no bad thing to have the chance of putting their difficult legal problems before judges who are still among the most able in the world. But there have been tensions, for instance with Trinidad and Tobago unhappy at some Privy Council decisions curtailing their right to execute convicted murderers. However, as the influence of the Privy Council wanes in respect of Britain's former possessions, it has been given a new role – to decide demarcation and constitutional disputes arising from the devolution of powers to Scotland, Wales and Northern Ireland.

The judges of the Privy Council are predominantly the same law lords that normally sit in the House of Lords, with the addition, every now and again, of eminent judges from Commonwealth countries.

## Tribunals

Outside the normal hierarchy of the courts flourishes a parallel structure of administrative and judicial bodies lumped together under the general description of tribunals. Some of them have been in existence for a century or more, but they have proliferated especially in the last 50 years, since the creation of the welfare state. The 80 or so tribunals cover a wide range of subjects, from tax to mental health. Some of the most important, and widely used, are the employment tribunals (which used to be called industrial tribunals), where workers can claim compensation for unfair dismissal or discrimination; the immigration appeals tribunal; and tribunals on supplementary benefits, rent, VAT, income tax, transport and dozens of other subjects.

The tribunals differ in their membership and rules of procedure, but they all conduct themselves according to the principles of justice used by the courts, especially in that the individuals appearing before them must have a chance to put their case.

## Employment Appeal Tribunal

The Employment Appeal Tribunal (EAT) was set up following the great increase of disputes arising from employment, especially involvpb0717$$$2g unfair dismissal or discrimination. The EAT hears appeals from employment tribunals. Every case is heard by a High Court judge and two lay members chosen for their knowledge and experience of industrial relations: trades union officials, for instance, and representatives of employers' organizations.

## Coroners' courts

Coroners, who must be qualified lawyers or doctors, have a duty to hold public inquests into any violent, unnatural or suspicious death, or in the case of a person dying suddenly without any obvious cause, or in prison or police custody. Coroners' inquests are not trials, but witnesses are called and there is often a jury which decides on the manner of death – suicide, unlawful killing, misadventure, accident – or, where there is uncertainty, returns an open verdict.

# The European Court of Justice

The European Court (more properly the Court of Justice of the European Communities) sits in Luxembourg. It is the court of the European Union, and therefore the United Kingdom, as a member, is under its jurisdiction on matters affecting the EU.

Its decisions on the interpretation of Community law (it's still called that, not Union law) are the last word in that area of the law, superior even to the pronouncements of the House of Lords. Its rulings, to date, have mainly concerned issues important to the business world but it has also given decisions of great importance to individuals, such as its ruling that women had the right to go on working to the same retirement age as men and other crucial decisions on sex equality and equal pay. Its power is demonstrated by the ruling which said that the UK government had been wrong in refusing certain Spanish fishermen access to waters near the UK; as a result, the UK had to pay tens of millions of pounds in compensation to the Spaniards for denying them their fishing rights.

# The European Court of Human Rights

The European Court of Human Rights sits in Strasbourg and operates under the umbrella of the Council of Europe, an organization with more than 40 member states. As its name suggests, the court deals with issues of human rights. It gives rulings on whether particular conduct by a government or one of its organs violates the European Convention on Human Rights, which the UK has signed. The court has made a number of rulings against the UK government on the rights of mental patients, prisoners and immigrants; and on such diverse topics as the right not to be caned at school, not to belong to a trades union, and freedom of expression. In 1998 the way the court operated was radically streamlined and made more efficient in order to get rid of the long delays in cases reaching it – sometimes six years. Its judges are now full-time and its procedures quicker.

The court, however, may not be as important as it used to be for Britons complaining that their rights were breached. As from October 2000, the European Convention on Human Rights will fully be part of the UK's national law, under the Human Rights Act 1998. This will mean that it will no longer be necessary to make the journey to Strasbourg to get a ruling from the court there – in future, UK judges will be able to take the decisions in our own courts. The Strasbourg court will still be the final court on human rights issues, but it's expected that many fewer UK cases will land up there.

# CHAPTER III

# The Lawyers

To the rest of the world, the English legal profession is a very strange species indeed. Most countries manage to do with one kind of lawyer. We, and a few other places which historically came under our influence, have two. Barristers and solicitors are usually thought of – and speak of themselves – as the two branches of a single legal profession. On closer examination, they really function as two separate professions, with different traditions, training and rules of conduct, and administered by separate governing bodies, but with a common body of knowledge, the law, and a common arena of operation, the courts.

Why two kinds of lawyer? As with so many of the legal profession's odd quirks, the reason for the division is historical, but (subject to a few demarcation disputes) it suited both branches of the profession for many years to maintain it, as proof against encroachment on each other's work. In the 1970s and into the 1980s debate raged over whether the two branches should be fused. By the late 1990s most of the restrictive practices which reserved particular areas of work for one branch or the other had been stripped away by successive governments, blurring the lines between the two to such an extent that the debate over fusion, which had become a dead issue, revived again.

The forerunners of today's barristers and solicitors were a mixed bunch, with varying titles and functions over the centuries. As long ago as the thirteenth century there were lawyers whose job was to plead in the King's courts on behalf of litigants, and court officials who acted as 'attorneys', providing general help to people involved in court proceedings, including appearing in court. Pleaders (barristers and serjeants) and attorneys both pleaded in court and both received clients direct. After lawyers organized themselves into the Inns of

Court in the mid-fourteenth century, there was a gradual separation of functions. Eventually attorneys were excluded from the Inns, and the higher courts came to be reserved for barristers and serjeants. In the meantime, other types of lawyers had appeared on the scene. Solicitors were concerned with property work and the chancery courts. Cases in chancery could drag on for generations, and the only way of moving matters forward was to employ someone to 'solicit' or cajole the court into getting on with things. Yet another legal functionary, the proctor, operated in the ecclesiastical and admiralty courts.

At first the solicitor was considered inferior to the attorney, but gradually their relative status was reversed, as solicitors' responsibility for land dealings made them the trusted advisers of the powerful landowning class. In 1875 the functions of solicitors, proctors and attorneys were merged, and the single title of solicitor was adopted. Serjeants were abolished too, leaving only barristers to represent that branch of the profession.

## Barristers

The Bar is the most traditional of professions. What other line of work requires its practitioners to spend much of their working lives kitted out in period costume? In London, barristers are still concentrated in the same offices (called 'chambers') in the Inns of Court – Gray's Inn, Lincoln's Inn, the Inner Temple and the Middle Temple – which have housed them since the fourteenth century, though lack of space and high rents have led many sets of chambers to relocate outside the Inns. Until very recently no one could qualify as a barrister without eating the required number of dinners in the Inns' dining hall (a tradition dating from Elizabethan times, before the introduction of formal legal education, when the theory was that the embryo lawyer would imbibe his elders' experience along with the equally well-aged claret). Now a number of the dinners can be replaced by attendance at weekend courses or education days.

Solicitors, accountants, surveyors and other professionals make contracts with their clients to provide services, and can sue those who are recalcitrant in paying their fees. Not so the barrister. Historically, he worked not for a fee, but for an 'honorarium'. Hence the pocket flap which still survives at the back of the barrister's gown, into which at one time the satisfied client would slip a token of his gratitude, without ever having to raise the sordid subject of money in conversation.

Although they cannot enter into contracts with clients, barristers are permitted to make contracts with solicitors but usually choose not to do so. Practice at the Bar is governed by an assortment of such customs, conventions and rules of etiquette of varying degrees of antiquity.

The Bar is regulated by a strict code of conduct. One of the most important principles is known as the 'cab-rank rule'. This is meant to ensure that everyone who needs a lawyer – even the most unpopular IRA terrorist or child molester – should have someone to champion his cause. Broadly, it says that a barrister must take any case he is offered, as long as it is within his usual sphere of practice, he is not otherwise engaged, and a proper fee is tendered. But the rule is almost impossible to police and, in practice, successful barristers pick and choose their cases with an eye to maximizing their income and furthering their careers.

Who are the barristers, and what distinguishes them from solicitors? Historically, as the senior branch of the profession, barristers came from a higher social class, but today both branches draw most of their recruits from the middle classes. The most common route to practice for both branches is a law degree followed by a year's professional course. Would-be solicitors must spend two years as trainees before qualifying. Barristers are called to the Bar when they pass their professional examination but must complete two six-month pupillages – traineeships – under a more senior barrister before they can qualify for a 'tenancy' – a permanent place to practise in chambers. For those without family money, the solicitors' branch is easier to get a start in, because the Law Society, the solicitors' professional body, insists that trainees are paid a minimum salary, while Bar pupils need not be paid at all. Because barristers are independent practitioners – unlike solicitors, who are permitted to practise in firms and are paid a salary from the start – a newly qualified barrister may struggle to find work and earn fees.

The Bar is the smaller branch of the profession: there are around 85,000 practising solicitors compared to some 9,000 barristers in private practice. Traditionally, solicitors were general practitioners who looked after their clients' day-to-day legal needs, and called on a barrister for anything difficult or if litigation was in the offing. A client who wanted to use a barrister's services could do so only through a solicitor. Solicitors did the office-based legal work, such as property conveyancing, making wills and winding up estates. Solicitors acted as advocates alongside barristers in the magistrates' and county courts. But advocacy in the Crown Court and the higher civil courts was reserved solely for barristers.

There are no simple analogies with other professions to explain the differences between solicitors and barristers. The often-cited comparison between general practitioners and hospital consultants in the medical profession was never true. The medical consultant becomes a specialist through years of extra training, whereas barristers receive no more training than solicitors. Though many barristers specialize in particular areas of law, many practise across a number of fields. Solicitors may also be specialists or generalists. The Bar's claim to be specialist advocates in the higher courts rests on the fact that, until recently, only the Bar had the right to appear in those courts.

The picture is now much more complicated. Both branches have become much more specialized in response to the growing complexity of the law, and barristers' privileges have been whittled away over the last decade. Change came, first, from the determination of government, both Conservative and Labour, to end what it saw as restrictive practices keeping the cost of legal services high and, second, from the Bar's need to adapt to the growing tendency for solicitors' firms to rely more on their own expertise and less on the Bar.

The Courts and Legal Services Act 1990 abolished the Bar's most cherished privilege – its exclusive right to conduct cases in the Crown Court, High Court and appeal courts. This monopoly had evolved from an old common-law rule that the courts can decide for themselves who could appear before them; by convention the higher courts reserved the right for barristers. As a result of the 1990 Act, the first solicitor advocates were licensed to take their place beside barristers in the higher courts of England and Wales in 1994. In Scotland reform has been swifter, with the first solicitors appearing in the higher courts in 1993.

Threatened with a massive shake-up by the 1989 government Green Paper on reform of the legal profession, which prefigured the 1990 Act, the Bar moved to liberalize many of its long-entrenched rules and practices. It remains a referral profession, its clients coming largely via solicitors, but an exception has been made for certain professions, including accountants and surveyors, who may now consult a barrister without a solicitor intermediary. In the late 1990s the rule was liberalized further to allow Citizens' Advice Bureaux to consult barristers direct, and BarDirect, a pilot scheme set up in 1999, has opened the direct route to organizations such as police forces, trades unions, professional organizations and doctors' defence bodies.

Barristers are now allowed to advertise their services and the fees they charge. They are no longer restricted to working from chambers, with a clerk, but may practise from home without a clerk after the first three years. Until fairly recently, barristers could not discuss fees with solicitors – negotiations had to be handled by the solicitor's clerk. A solicitor who wanted a barrister's advice had to go to the barrister; only exceptionally would a barrister set foot in a solicitor's office. Such conventions have been swept away as the Bar has responded to a changing market, including the increasing size and expertise of solicitors' firms and the trend for solicitors to keep in-house work which once would have gone to the Bar.

In the past, the Bar was drawn mainly from Oxbridge and the public schools. But a flick through Bar directories shows those with Oxbridge degrees to be in a minority today.

In recent years the acute shortage of openings at the Bar, the uncertain level of earnings in the first few years, and the prospect of intellectually challenging work and high financial rewards in the large commercial law firms, have attracted to the solicitors' branch many high-quality graduates who, in the past, might have opted for the Bar.

Qualifying as a barrister now requires at least a second-class degree, though not necessarily in law. The would-be barrister must join one of the Inns of Court: it is the Inn which calls practitioners to the Bar.

During their year's Bar vocational course, aspiring barristers participate in role-playing and practical exercises conducted by experienced barristers. The training is run on modern lines, contrary to the old-fashioned image the profession presents. The course concentrates on the practical skills of advocacy, negotiation and drafting that the new barrister will need in practice. Assessors mark students on their live performance as advocates and negotiators.

Passing the Bar exams and being called to the Bar are just the beginning. A barrister who wants to practise at the Bar must do two six-month pupillages in chambers, sitting in on conferences with his 'pupil master' (a more senior barrister), sitting in court, looking up points of law, doing some paperwork, and generally learning the tricks of the trade. Pupillages have traditionally been unpaid, although many are now 'funded', guaranteeing the pupil's earnings up to a fixed level. During the second six months the young barrister may take on work of his own – if he is lucky enough to get any.

Unpaid pupillages – together with the lack of local authority grants for Bar school – have biased entry towards those from better-off families. The Bar has attempted to remedy this by asking chambers to guarantee a minimum £10,000 a year during pupillage. Entry to the profession is insecure because not every graduate from the Bar vocational course will get pupillage. In 1999–2000 there were 2,018 applications under the Bar's pupillage clearing house scheme (PACH) for 671 advertised pupillages – only 226 of them funded. And there is no guarantee that the pupil will be able to stay in the same chambers after pupillage is over. The barrister can practise only if he is offered a 'seat' or 'tenancy' in a set of chambers. The number of candidates considerably outstrips the vacancies available. In 1998–9 only 476 new barristers obtained a tenancy, down from 543 the previous year and 615 the year before. Eventually, many abandon the Bar, taking jobs in business, the civil service or outside the law, or switching over to the solicitors' branch.

In the past, getting a pupillage or a seat in chambers was a question of who you knew rather than what you knew – connections rather than merit. Some young barristers argue that this is still the case. In recent years the Bar has adopted an equality code, designed to ensure that pupillages and tenancies are allocated on merit and not on connections, and has tried to ensure fairness through its PACH scheme. But the system is not compulsory and some of the top chambers have bypassed it and headhunted star students direct. Sir Stephen Sedley, an Appeal Court judge, in a lecture in September 1999 described the end-product as 'a reproach to the profession' and 'an inadequate and unfair allocation of pupillages'. Sir Stephen warned:

The most serious consequence of the present situation is that the Bar's intake risks reverting to what it was at the beginning of the century: a social, economic and racial elite.

Even the fortunate few who secure tenancies can by no means look forward to an assured future. Every barrister is a self-employed, independent operator. Unlike newly qualified solicitors, who are paid a salary and given work by their firm, fledgling barristers are expected to attract their own work and earn their own fees. In practice, they rely heavily on chambers clerks to suggest their names to solicitors ringing up to ask for someone appropriate to handle simple county court and magistrates' court work, and to persuade solicitors to substitute them if their first choice turns out to be otherwise engaged. Distinguished judges are fond of recalling how they were on the verge of leaving the Bar in desperation when the brief (the document by which solicitors hire barristers) came in that changed their luck. The coming of legal aid in 1950, however, relegated the briefless barrister to the ranks of fiction, and for the last 50 years public funds have provided a cushion – albeit, given the low fees payable to junior barristers for publicly funded work, a not very well stuffed one – against penury in the first few years. But with cutbacks in public funding and increasing competition from solicitors, young barristers are again facing a struggle for survival.

## Women

The proportion of women at the Bar is about 25 per cent – compared to about 35 per cent for solicitors – but growing. Of barristers aged 30 or under, or up to five years in practice, around 37 per cent are women. A 1992 survey by the Bar Council and the Lord Chancellor's Department found 'substantial evidence of early and continuing unequal treatment between the sexes at many levels of the profession'. Women had to make more applications for pupillages and undergo more interviews. More women 'squatted' in chambers, staying on informally after pupillage without an offer of a tenancy, and for a longer period. A 1995 study (by the University of Sheffield Institute for the Study of the Legal Profession) of barristers in their first few years of practice found that a majority of women had experienced sex discrimination: 56 per cent had slight problems and 16 per cent major problems. Women with the same number of years at the Bar are less likely to achieve the sought-after rank of Queen's Counsel (QC) – the top 10 per cent of the profession, who command the largest fees. Out of some 1100 QCs practising in April 2000, around 90 were women. However, in recent years the few women who have applied have had a higher success rate than the men. In the past some clerks and heads of chambers operated a quota system, claiming that solicitors didn't like briefing women barristers, or that women would let the chambers down by going off to start families. Too often, female barristers find themselves channelled into divorce and crime, the least intellectually challenging and least well paid areas of work. In 1993 the Bar adopted an equality code of practice to promote equal opportunities for women and ethnic minorities.

## The brief

In general, no one can retain a barrister's services except through a solicitor. There are limited exceptions for other professionals like accountants and surveyors, and the BarDirect scheme for direct access to certain organizations (*see* p. 38). But in the main, barristers rely for their work on what solicitors send them. Solicitors tend to have their favourite sets of chambers for particular types of work. Although the Bar no longer has a monopoly in the higher courts, most advocacy there will continue, at least for the foreseeable future, to be handled by barristers. In the county court or magistrates' court, a solicitor has the choice of acting as advocate himself or instructing a barrister. Practical considerations will decide which he chooses. If he has a string of clients appearing before the local magistrates on the same day, it might be more economical to represent them all himself. On the other hand, if a case involves an appearance before a distant county court, it might be cheaper to send along a young barrister, who will do it for a flat fee, less than the solicitor would have to charge for his own time.

The means of communication between solicitor and barrister is the brief, the document which tells the barrister what the solicitor wants him to do, and gives him all the information he needs to do the job. The barrister may be briefed to appear in court, or to give an opinion on a tricky point of law, or to draft pleadings (documents used in civil cases) or to advise on whether to accept an offer of settlement.

The brief to appear for the prosecution or defence in a criminal trial is the focus of one of the most vexed problems in the system – the late return of briefs. Because one trial will end earlier than expected and another will go on much longer, a clerk will often double-book a barrister, rather as travel agencies or airlines overbook, to make sure that he isn't left with an empty, and hence unpaid-for, day. The briefs that the barristers can't handle then have to be returned to be reallocated, often at the last minute and often to someone more junior. A survey of every Crown Court in February 1992 for the Royal Commission on Criminal Justice found that 59 per cent of prosecution briefs and 44 per cent of defence briefs in contested cases were returned briefs. Half of prosecuting barristers and one-third of defence barristers had received the brief only on the day of the hearing, or the day before. All this may seem sensible and efficient from the Bar's point of view, but it can be a disaster for the client, who has been told by his solicitor that a particular barrister is appearing, and comes to court to find another. Often defendants believe – sometimes justifiably – that the new counsel foisted on them is inferior, and doesn't properly know the case. It leads to bitterness and loss of confidence in the system of justice.

The difficulty is caused partly by the system of listing cases for trial. To make maximum use of court time, the listing officials have to show great flexibility in juggling cases around. This means that a barrister often gets only a day or two's notice of the day of the trial, and he may be involved in another case.

The relationship between solicitor and barrister largely excludes the individual client. He cannot see or contact the barrister directly, only through his solicitor. There may be a meeting – a conference – between the client, his solicitor and his barrister before the trial, but most defendants in criminal cases meet their barrister for the first time on the day of the trial. The 1992 Crown Court survey found that over half of those pleading guilty, and almost 70 per cent of those who changed their plea to guilty on the day, met their barristers only on the morning of the trial. Almost one-third of defendants replying to the Crown Court survey said they had not had enough time with their barrister, although only one in ten barristers felt that the time was insufficient.

A National Audit Office study of Crown Courts in 1997 found that prosecution briefs were returned to the Crown Prosecution Service (CPS) in three-quarters of cases and, in almost one-third of those, the substitute was 'judged to have been of inappropriate quality'. In some cases, the then Director of Public Prosecutions, Dame Barbara Mills, told MPs, barristers were returning the briefs because better-paid work had come up. From February 1999 a system for monitoring the reasons for returned briefs was set up, with the ultimate sanction of barring offending chambers from CPS work. But a CPS Inspectorate report in February 2000 found that briefs were returned in 50 per cent of cases, sometimes the night before a trial, and judges were concerned about the quality of substitutes.

## Earnings

A barrister's earnings will increase as he gains experience and takes on more weighty work, though how much he earns will depend on his own ability, how hard he is willing to work, and the area of law he practises in. Barristers are divided into two tiers: QCs (Queen's Counsel) and juniors. All barristers who are not QCs are called juniors, regardless of their age or seniority. The successful junior, after around 15–20 years' practice, may apply to become a QC or 'take silk' (so called because the QC wears a silk gown). Seventy-eight new silks were appointed in 2000, around 15.4 per cent of those who applied. Some are turned down several times before they make it, while others never succeed and eventually stop applying. The process of selection is carried out by the Lord Chancellor and his senior officials via confidential consultations with the judges and senior barristers and solicitors. It operates in much the same way as the method of choosing High Court judges (*see* Chapter IV). There are growing pressures on the Lord Chancellor to reform the system, which is much criticized for being anachronistic, unaccountable and discriminatory against women, ethnic minorities and solicitors. The rank of QC was opened to solicitors in 1990 but by 2000 only four had qualified. In 1999 the Law Society, the solicitors' professional body, decided to stop co-operating with the 'secret soundings' system for selecting both QCs and judges.

Queen's Counsel are traditionally the top 10 per cent or so of the Bar – there are around 1100 of them – and they form the pool from which most High Court judges are drawn. Taking silk brings increased status, higher fees, and the chance to get rid of a heavy load of paperwork. A QC appearing in court will usually have a junior helping him. Until 1977, the Bar's rules of conduct prevented a QC from working without a junior. Although the rule was dropped, following a Monopolies Commission finding that it was against the public interest, QCs still work with a junior's assistance in most cases. So not only does the client have to pay the higher fees due to a QC, he has to pay for two barristers instead of one – plus, of course, the solicitor.

The risk in taking silk is that not enough clients will want to pay so much more, and a previously flourishing career may stagnate. But a 1999 survey by management consultants BDO Stoy Hayward, the first reliable survey of the Bar's earnings, found that one in four silks earned more than £266,000 a year in net fees – after expenses (averaging 23.4 per cent), but before deducting pension contributions, national insurance or tax. In 1999, 20 silks were reckoned by Chambers' *Guide to the Legal Profession* to belong to the 'million-a-year club', earning gross fees of £1 million or more. Specialist, commercial and chancery (including disputes about trusts and land) QCs are the top earners and over a quarter of the list of 20 are tax lawyers. Commercial, chancery and specialist barristers earn twice as much on average as those practising in the fields of crime and family law, who draw most of their income from state funds. Queen's Counsel paid purely from the public purse, for prosecuting or defending in criminal cases, or for representing people in state-funded civil cases, still earn substantial incomes – more than any other profession paid by the taxpayer. Figures released by the Lord Chancellor in the late 1990s showed that QCs representing people who have suffered devastating injuries in medical negligence cases and those appearing in child care cases can pull in £300,000 or more in a good year, and £500,000 is not unknown among QCs who defend in big fraud cases. The days of such high earnings from public funds are numbered, however; the Lord Chancellor is taking steps to curb excessive fees and is cracking down on the unnecessary use of QCs, and of two barristers where one would do.

At the other end of the earnings spectrum, many barristers embarking on their careers are poorly paid and struggle to find enough work. One in four of those in the first five years of practice netted less than £17,000 after expenses in 1998–99, according to the BDO Stoy Hayward survey. But the top quarter of those in the first five years netted more than £42,700.

## Organization

Unlike solicitors, barristers are not allowed to practise in partnership or share fees. Each barrister remains an independent contractor. But they cluster together in sets of chambers, sharing clerks, libraries and administrative back-up. In 1999 a typical barrister operated from chambers with about 25 members, though a wave of mergers is rapidly producing bigger sets.

In London, chambers are concentrated in the four Inns of Court:

Lincoln's Inn, Gray's Inn, Inner Temple and Middle Temple, although there is a growing trend to relocate in office buildings just outside the Inns. Each set has its head, usually a senior QC, and is administered by a clerk, a practice manager or both. The members contribute, usually in proportion to their earnings, to running expenses, rent, heat and light, typists' salaries and clerks' pay. Barristers' overheads, including personal expenses, generally work out at slightly less than one-quarter of their gross fees.

No one knows exactly when the four Inns of Court were established, but they were already a going concern in the fourteenth century. Originally medieval guilds of lawyers, they appear to have served as residential clubs for lawyers and places where students came to learn the law. Stepping from the bustle of Fleet Street into the courtyards and lawns of the Temple is like taking a trip backwards in time. Though some of the buildings are post-war, rebuilt following bomb damage, the new blends inconspicuously with the old, leaving an impression of a beautiful but cloistered and anachronistic world.

Every student has to join an Inn, and he remains a member of that Inn throughout his life at the Bar and on the bench, if he becomes a judge. Members lunch and dine in their Inns and use their libraries. It is the Benchers (governing members) of the Inns who call a student to the Bar.

Barristers practising outside London are much less cloistered. They tend to be grouped together in smaller chambers, in run-of-the-mill office buildings near the court, not set apart from the rest in their own little world.

The Bar Council is the barristers' elected representative body. It determines policy, sets the standards and ethics of professional conduct, and represents generally the interests of its members – the nearest equivalent of a trades union for barristers.

## Complaints against barristers

Far fewer complaints are made against barristers than against solicitors, reflecting the fact that the great bulk of legal work is handled by solicitors. Most complaints about barristers relate to their conduct of cases in court. The Bar Council will consider complaints of either inadequate professional service – such as delays, poor work on a case, rudeness to the client – or professional misconduct, such as misleading the court or breaching confidentiality. Some complaints may initially be referred for conciliation between the barrister and the client. Complaints are investigated by the complaints commissioner, who is not a lawyer. If he thinks it should be taken further, he refers it to the Bar Council's professional conduct and complaints committee, which may dismiss it if the two lay members agree, or refer it on for a decision on whether the complaint is justified. Decisions on inadequate professional service complaints are taken by an adjudication panel of two practising barristers and a lay representative chaired by the commissioner. A barrister found guilty may be required to apologize, forgo some or all of the fees due, or pay compensation up to £5000. Some professional misconduct cases are dealt with by a panel, which can admonish the barrister if not satisfied with his explanation. A summary hearing panel, which deals with more serious cases where there is no dispute about the facts, can impose fines up to £500 or suspend the barrister for up to six months. The most serious cases are heard in public by a disciplinary tribunal – a panel of two barristers and two lay representatives, chaired by a judge. The tribunal has a range of penalties, including suspension for any period, a fine of up to £5000 payable to the Bar Council, and the ultimate sanction, disbarment. Tribunals and panels considering misconduct allegations may also consider claims of inadequate professional services and order the appropriate remedies.

Like solicitors, barristers can be sued for negligence in out-of-court work, but neither a solicitor nor a barrister can be sued over his performance as an advocate in court or work closely connected with the advocacy.

## Barristers' clerks

The senior barristers' clerk is a powerful figure, 'a complicated cross between a theatrical agent, a business manager, an accountant, and a trainer', in the words of Sir Robert Megarry, a former head of the

High Court's Chancery Division. The clerk negotiates the barristers' fees and to a large extent can make or break the career of the young barrister by diverting work to him or away from him. In many chambers the clerk will have a say in whether or not a new member is taken on.

Yet the clerk has no legal qualifications, and in many cases will have begun straight from school as a junior clerk, carrying books and running errands, gradually working his way up to a position of power and influence – and a level of earnings – out of all proportion to his academic attainments.

Traditionally, senior clerks were paid a straight percentage of the gross fees of the barristers they served, between five and ten per cent. As chambers expanded in size, so clerks' earnings grew. The biggest sets of chambers now have more than 70 members. Many senior clerks earn six-figure sums, more than many of the barristers they work for. Attempts to put them on a straight salary have largely failed and only about 15 per cent of senior clerks in London chambers were paid this way in 1999. The most common method of payment is a salary plus a commission based on a percentage of fees. Jobs advertised in 1999 offered packages worth between £60,000 and £80,000. There is a growing trend for chambers to recruit practice managers or chambers directors to handle marketing, IT, finances and strategic planning, leaving the clerks to their traditional role of managing the barristers' work. Despite this trend, the traditional clerk still holds sway and the top rank of clerks in blue chip chambers earn well over £200,000 a year.

## Solicitors

It is a common fallacy that barristers spend all their time arguing in court while solicitors stay in their offices doing paperwork. Although many of the 85,000 or so practising solicitors will rarely venture inside a courtroom, others spend half or more of their working week in court. Conversely, some barristers spend the bulk of their time on paperwork.

## What they do

As the first port of call for anyone with a legal problem, the average solicitor deals with a greater variety of work than the average barrister. Even when a barrister is involved in a case, most of the legal work is done by the solicitor. In a civil case, which may or may not go to court – such as a claim for damages for injuries in an accident – the solicitor does most of the preparatory work and conducts the negotiations which may lead to a settlement out of court. The barrister may be called in by the solicitor to draft the court paperwork – though many solicitors in larger firms will do their own – to advise, and to appear in court if the case gets that far. In the bigger solicitors' firms, barristers are called in less than they used to be in the past.

Most criminal cases are handled from start to finish by solicitors in the magistrates' court, though some solicitors, particularly in London, make it a practice to instruct a junior barrister for the court hearing. More serious crimes are tried in the Crown Court, where the Bar, until recently, had a monopoly on advocacy rights. Solicitors had just started to make inroads on Crown Court advocacy by early 2000. The courts, though, are just the tip of the legal iceberg. Most legal work never, or rarely, involves the courts. Solicitors divide their work into 'contentious work' and 'non-contentious work'. Anything which involves court proceedings is contentious; examples include crime, divorce, and civil litigation (such as claims for damages in accident cases). Everything else is non-contentious. Many firms still act as general practitioners or family solicitors, dealing with the complete range of their clients' legal problems, but there is a strong trend towards specialization and firms are growing larger.

At one time the less profitable contentious work was heavily subsidized by the non-contentious, particularly conveyancing. But moves in Parliament to smash the solicitors' monopoly on conveyancing work and open it up to non-lawyers – culminating in legislation in 1985 allowing the licensing of conveyancers without legal qualifications – have resulted in fierce competition in the conveyancing market and brought fees down sharply. Solicitors have cut their margins to compete not only with licensed conveyancers, who, as a result, have not made great inroads into the solicitors' traditional preserve, but more particularly with each other. In 1967 the profession derived 50 per cent of its income from the conveyancing of residential property. Today, only about 12 per cent of the typical firm's income comes from this source. This decline in a traditionally profitable area has been coupled with a squeeze on the fees earned from legal aid work, which, at the best of times, was never a high-profit activity. State-funded work is likely to account for a decreasing proportion of solicitors' income with the removal of aid from personal injury cases in April 2000, as well as the concentration of such work in fewer firms and the introduction of a more stringent code for granting aid.

## Structure and earnings

Solicitors practise on their own or in partnership, though for the first few years of working life a solicitor usually works as a salaried or 'assistant' solicitor. The Law Society's rules prohibit a solicitor from setting up as a sole practitioner for three years after admission. Full partners or 'equity' partners own a share of the firm and share the profits. Each partner in a firm is fully liable for the debts or negligent acts of the other partners. Most solicitors' firms are small businesses. More than 40 per cent of firms are headed by a sole practitioner – a solicitor on his own, with no partners. Four out of five firms have fewer than five partners and only five per cent of firms have more than ten partners.

The usual route into the profession is through a law degree. Although a degree of any sort is not compulsory, about 98 per cent of entrants are graduates, not all in law. For the law graduate there is a further one year's practical course and examination. The non-law graduate needs an extra year before that.

The aspiring solicitor serves for two years as a trainee solicitor, earning a small salary – the minimum from August 2000 will be £12,000 outside London, £13,600 in the capital, though the lucky few chosen by the big City firms can start on around £21,000, rising to £24,000 in the second year. During this time, the trainee progresses from carrying out simple research, one-off drafting tasks, and 'supporting counsel' (sitting behind a barrister in court) to seeing his own cases through from start to finish. In the 1980s newly qualified solicitors were in a seller's market, with jobs easy to come by and good candidates able to pick and choose. A recession in the nineties changed the picture, but by 2000 prospects had improved again, with a reasonable balance between candidates and traineeships or jobs for the newly qualified.

Once the assistant solicitor has proved himself, he can hope to be offered a partnership. This means that he will get a share of the firm's profits instead of a salary. The length of time it takes to become a partner will depend on luck, ability, the size of the firm, the area of work and the part of the country in which a solicitor practises. Outside London he should make it within five years: in some areas or firms much sooner. In the big City of London firms, 35 is reckoned to be the make or break age for a partnership. Those who fail to make the grade generally move to a smaller firm with better partnership prospects.

The typical solicitor is aged around 40, is white, male and the product of a middle-class home. Women made up 35 per cent of the practising profession in 1999, though the picture is changing rapidly. Of those joining the profession in 1998–9, 52.6 per cent were women. In the past, women have experienced difficulties in obtaining partnerships ('they'll just go off and have babies'), but this too is changing, and most of the large London firms now have several women partners. However, Law Society statistics show that women are less likely to become partners and tend to be paid less than men.

As at the Bar, there is a wide gulf in the solicitors' branch between the highest and lowest earners. It is extremely difficult to discuss 'average' or 'typical' earnings. The range is immense but, as a rule of thumb, the bigger the firm the higher the earnings. The Law Society regularly monitors the structure, work and finances of a representative panel of 554 firms around England and Wales. At one end of the spectrum is the solicitor practising on his own or in a small country partnership; at the other are senior partners in the large commercial firms. The autumn 1998 survey found that one in four sole practitioners earned less than £25,000. The typical sole practitioner made profits of £44,000. The middle of the range for equity partners (those sharing in the profits) ranged from £52,000 per partner in a two to four partner firm to £178,000 in a firm of 26–80 partners.

At the top of the earnings scale, and excluded from the Law Society survey, are the huge firms, mainly in the City, with 100 or more partners and hundreds of assistant solicitors. Clifford Chance, the largest firm in the world after a merger with a US and a German firm, has more than 550 partners and 3000 lawyers. Some 24 other firms have more than 80 partners. Mega-firms are no longer the exclusive preserve of the City. A number of provincial firms have moved into the 50-partner-plus category. The biggest now operate from London as well as provincial centres and compete successfully with the traditional City firms for highly paid commercial work. The last 10 years have seen several of the bigger provincial firms turn into national firms.

The huge commercial firms serve the legal needs of big business and finance: the conveyancing of office blocks, business disputes involving large sums of money, company flotations, mergers, takeovers, tax, banking, insurance and so on. Each partner and solicitor specializes.

In 2000 the biggest city firms raised pay for newly qualified solicitors to £42,000. In the Law Society's autumn 1998 panel survey, one in four firms in the 26–80 partner category garnered profits of more than £332,000 per partner. Not all the profits will be taken as pay by the partners; some will remain in the business as working capital. A few top partners in large commercial firms notch up profits nearing £1 million a year, thanks to a boom in corporate work.

In addition to the big City firms, London has a large number of medium-sized firms (20–50 partners). Some firms specialize in particular areas of law, such as shipping, entertainment, trades unions, media law and copyright and insurance. The old established discreet upper-crust family firms with rich private clients are still there, but are increasingly having to find additional areas of work to keep them in the style to which they are accustomed.

The most significant trend in recent years has been on the merger front. At all levels, in London and in the provinces, firms have amalgamated. Sometimes the merger has been between equals; other mergers have been more like takeovers, with one firm swallowing up another. Outside London, there have been a number of mergers or looser associations between firms in different cities and towns, with the intention of creating what amounts to region-wide, or even nationwide, firms. Not all mergers are successful, but the drive to become bigger looks likely to continue to be an important element in the structure of the solicitors' profession.

Outside private practice, the Law Society estimates that somewhere in the region of 16,000 men and women are employed as solicitors in commerce and industry, and in central and local government, including the Crown Prosecution Service. Building societies, finance houses, insurance companies, property companies and large companies of all sorts increasingly employ in-house lawyers in the American mould, to advise the company on the legality of its proposed activities, do its conveyancing and litigation, act as company secretaries, and brief lawyers in private practice where necessary. Solicitors in local government provide a similar sort of service to the elected council. The chief executive of a local authority is often a solicitor, and company lawyers often move into management. Solicitors in industry often do better financially than those in private practice, taking into account pensions and other perks which solicitors in private practice have to provide out of their earnings.

## Organization

The Law Society is the solicitors' professional association, which seeks to advance the interests of the profession. But the Law Society has much wider functions, and controls the education of solicitors, their admission to the profession and their right to practise. To obtain the annual practising certificate – the licence to practise issued by the Law Society – a solicitor must have indemnity insurance of up to £1 million per transaction and file an annual accountant's report.

## Complaints against solicitors

Complaints are dealt with by the Office for the Supervision of Solicitors (OSS), set up in 1996 as a successor to the Solicitors' Complaints Bureau. The bureau had been founded as a semi-independent body in 1986 in response to what the Royal Commission on Legal Services described in 1979 as 'a general feeling of unease about the Law Society's handling of complaints, a feeling that "lawyers look after their own"'.

Neither the bureau nor the OSS has managed to inspire public confidence in the system. The OSS was set up largely because the bureau had become discredited through delays and inefficiency, but its own performance has proved so poor that, in the Access to Justice Act 1999, the government took powers, held in reserve for the moment, to hand over the regulation of solicitors to an outside regulator. If the OSS fails to meet targets set by management consultants Ernst & Young to clear its backlog by the end of 2000 and, thereafter, resolve 90 per cent of complaints within three months, the Lord Chancellor has threatened to give the task to a new regulatory body. The Law Society injected an extra £5.7 million into the complaints system in 1999 in line with Ernst & Young's blueprint for bringing the system up to scratch.

Since 1991 solicitors' firms have been required to set up their own in-house complaints procedures. Disgruntled clients are supposed to try to resolve their complaints with the solicitor first before involving the OSS. But solicitors have by no means embraced the customer culture found in big companies. Law Society research on the OSS's predecessor, the Solicitors' Complaints Bureau, published in 1996, found that 'satisfaction levels with both the outcome of the complaint dealt with by the solicitor and with the solicitor's overall complaints handling were very poor.' Only three per cent of one sample and eight per cent of another sample said their solicitor had done something to resolve their complaint.

Most complaints fall into the category of 'inadequate professional services'. Delays, failure to respond to telephone calls or letters, failure to follow instructions and overcharging were the largest areas of complaint in the 1996 survey. The OSS can order a solicitor to forgo all or part of his fees and can award compensation of up to £5000.

The OSS also deals with allegations of professional misconduct against solicitors. These include such misdeeds as breaching an undertaking to do something, or acting for two parties with conflicting interests. Where a solicitor has breached a rule of conduct, the bureau can rebuke him, attach conditions to his practising certificate – for example, requiring him to practise only with a partner – or prohibit him from taking on a trainee.

Charges of serious professional misconduct go to the independent Solicitors' Disciplinary Tribunal, which has lay representation. It can order a solicitor to be suspended or struck off.

Clients dissatisfied with the way the OSS has dealt with their complaint can ask the Legal Services Ombudsman to review it. The ombudsman can recommend further action, including the payment of compensation by the solicitor or by the OSS. In her 1999 annual report, the current ombudsman, Ann Abraham, castigated the Law Society for a 'catalogue of failures' in its complaints handling system. She criticized solicitors for 'delaying tactics, pedantry and rampant obstructiveness' when dealing with complaints in-house.

## Reform

The 1970s saw growing criticism of the structure and monopolies of the legal profession. Critics questioned the rationale behind the divided legal profession, arguing that fusion of barristers and solicitors into one profession would reduce double-manning and cut the costs of court cases. After one lawyer, the solicitor, had involved himself in the case, become familiar with the details, and developed a relationship with the client, it was said, the case had to be handed over to another lawyer, the barrister. He, in turn, had to spend costly time familiarizing himself with the case.

Opponents of fusion argued that doing away with the division would not necessarily lead to reduced duplication and lower costs. There would always be the need for one lawyer to prepare the case and another to handle it in court, and some degree of duplication would be inevitable. If the lawyer preparing the case was not a specialist, bringing in an outsider who could isolate the legal problems and solve them more quickly would save costs. In court the expert advocate would be less verbose and know the points to concentrate on, making the trial shorter, cheaper and more likely to be successful.

Both branches of the profession opposed fusion, and the Royal Commission on Legal Services, which reported in 1979, decided it would dilute the standard of advocacy and act against the public interest. The Law Society, however, began to press for rights for solicitors to appear as advocates in the higher courts. The Bar was adamantly opposed. Into the resulting deadlock stepped Lord Mackay, appointed Lord Chancellor in 1987. A Scottish advocate and son of a railway worker, he had none of his predecessors' traditional loyalties to the English Bar. The Conservative government had pledged itself to end restrictive practices and some of the most obvious, including the Bar's monopoly on higher court rights of audience and High Court judgeships, operated within the legal profession.

To the dismay of the Bar and the judges, Lord Mackay issued a Green Paper in 1989 with a much more radical package of proposals than either branch of the profession had expected. Solicitors were to be given the right to appear in all courts, right up to the House of Lords, and to become eligible for even the highest judicial appointments. Crown Prosecution Service lawyers were to be allowed to conduct their own cases in the Crown Courts, clients were to have direct access to barristers without going through a solicitor, and the way was paved for mixed partnerships of barristers, solicitors and other professionals.

After five months of intense lobbying by the Bar and judges, the final proposals, incorporated in the Courts and Legal Services Act 1990, were less radical. Direct access to barristers and mixed partnerships were scrapped. A complex and bureaucratic procedure was set up under which solicitors and CPS lawyers might eventually win audience rights in the higher courts. Applications by professional bodies such as the Law Society for extended advocacy rights had to be approved by an advisory committee and were subject to a veto by any one of four senior judges. The Law Society's proposal for private practice solicitors was approved in late 1993, and in 1994 the first few solicitors were licensed to appear in the Crown Court, High Court or both. By 2000 around 1000 solicitors had qualified and several of the big City law firms were doing a significant proportion of their own advocacy.

But there was a lengthy battle over rights for barristers and solicitors in the CPS to conduct their own cases in the Crown Court – seen as a much more significant threat to the Bar's livelihood. Barristers and judges argued that state employees would not be sufficiently independent, despite the fact that prosecutors in virtually every other country in the world are public employees. Solicitors employed outside private practice eventually won the right to appear in the higher courts but only as juniors to a more senior advocate.

Labour came to power in 1997, and the new Lord Chancellor, Lord Irvine, lost patience and dismantled the machinery which had hampered further progress, opening the way to full advocacy rights for all CPS and other employed lawyers.

In opposing the original proposals, the Bar claimed they would lead inevitably to fusion, with the best barristers being snapped up as advocates by the big City solicitors' firms. The Bar, its leaders argued, would no longer survive as a separate entity.

Few doubt that the Bar will survive, albeit in a slimmed-down form. What is undoubtedly true is that the traditional demarcation lines between the two branches have become substantially blurred and will fade further. Solicitors' firms are hiring barristers as in-house advocates, but mainly at the middle rather than the top level. By no means all of the changes can be attributed to the dismantling of restrictive practices, though the government's determination to open the higher courts to all lawyers should result in substantial inroads on what is still almost a Bar monopoly in the higher courts. The growth of solicitors' firms in size and specialization has meant that more specialist work is handled by solicitors, rather than the Bar. Reforms, in 1999, to the civil justice system following a blueprint by Lord Woolf, then Master of the Rolls, have prompted big litigation firms to do more of the barrister's traditional work in-house. The Bar has responded with a new scheme, BarDirect, allowing organizations such as the police, probation services, trades unions, and professional bodies to consult barristers direct, without a referral from a solicitor.

## The future

The trend towards larger law firms and more narrow specialization by solicitors means that many of the ablest specialists are now in the solicitors' branch. The market for barristers' services has shrunk as solicitors' firms become more specialized, handle more work in-house and send less to the Bar. Many barristers now believe the Bar will ultimately have to shrink rather than expand, and become a small cadre of specialists. Senior specialists still have plenty of work and the top QCs are highly sought after, but many feel that the shortage of work for junior barristers will make it hard for chambers to train and retain tomorrow's specialist QCs.

The importance of oral advocacy in the legal system is likely to diminish, with moves towards more written procedures and limits on time spent arguing cases in court, in line with the growing recognition that the traditional system has become too costly a way of settling disputes.

Barristers, unlike solicitors, are forbidden to operate in partnership with each other. Each barrister is an independent practitioner, but barristers' chambers are starting to develop a more corporate ethos, funding their pupils, providing chambers training and publishing marketing brochures. In the longer term, they could be permitted to practise as partners, and even to join firms of solicitors as partners. The increasing use of no-win, no-fee arrangements for funding litigation could hasten the coming of partnerships between barristers because chambers will have to agree to provide another barrister willing to work on the same basis if the first has to drop out. Whether this happens or not, it seems likely that the demarcation lines between the two branches of the divided profession will become increasingly blurred. Some believe that fusion may be on the far horizon.

# CHAPTER IV

# The Judges

The English judge, much respected and much satirized, is, to some people, the awesome embodiment of wisdom, independence and impartiality in a free society. To others he is an elderly, remote, crusty figure wearing ridiculous fancy dress, speaking strange jargon and holding views more appropriate to the nineteenth century. He has been much represented and misrepresented in literature, and on film and television, with the result that the public has a somewhat bizarre idea of who he is and what he does.

Until recently, English judges were bashful and reticent creatures, rarely emerging into public gaze, happy to do their work as unobtrusively as possible and disappear back into the rarefied, cocooned atmosphere of the Inns of Court. They tended to come into the public eye only if they did or said something in court which was silly or controversial, or when carrying out some important public function, like an inquiry into an issue of national importance. Examples include Lord Scarman's inquiry into the Brixton riots of 1981, Lord Justice Taylor on the safety of sports grounds following the Hillsborough disaster, Dame Elizabeth Butler-Sloss's 1988 inquiry into the Cleveland child sex abuse cases, and Lord Justice Scott's 1994 investigation of the background to the arms-for-Iraq affair. More recently, Lord Phillips has been looking into the BSE crisis and Lord Saville is reviewing the events in Londonderry on 'Bloody Sunday', 1972.

In the past few years, though, judges have become much more public figures. Until 1987, they were barred, or at least strongly discouraged, from speaking to the media 'on the record', giving interviews, participating in radio and television programmes, writing for newspapers or in other ways joining the public debate on contemporary issues. When Lord Mackay became Lord Chancellor he opened the door to allow judges greater freedom to express themselves publicly. The arrival of a media-friendly Lord Chief Justice, Lord Taylor, in 1992 added to the atmosphere of greater openness. As a result, it is now common to see, hear or read interviews with judges in which they are often critical and outspoken. Lord Taylor started the habit of giving press conferences, which his successor Lord Bingham continued. Taylor was even a panelist on TV's Question Time, although it was a specially restricted programme confined to questions about law and the legal system. At the other end of the spectrum, a relatively junior judge, Judge Matthewman, made history in 1993 by being given a regular television slot in which to express his views.

## The hierarchy

The first myth to be dispelled is that judges always wear the full-bottomed wigs in which they are often pictured in the newspapers or in news-films of the quaint ceremonies they attend. Full wigs are ceremonial only. In court they wear short versions which sit on the head rather than envelop it. And the most senior judges, the law lords, are not robed or wigged at all.

In 1993 the Lord Chancellor, Lord Mackay, reacting to suggestions from both within the legal world and outside it, conducted a survey among the judiciary, barristers and the public inquiring whether judicial wigs should be retained at all. Did they, as one side argued (including, perhaps surprisingly, many of the most senior judges), represent an unnecessary tradition that merely served to heighten people's feelings that judges were remote and out of touch? Or did the horsehair appendages serve to symbolize the authority and majesty of the law and increase respect for the judiciary? The inquiry concluded that the majority of judges, lawyers and the general public wanted the wigs to stay.

There are altogether more than 1100 full-time judges and more than 2000 part-time. The most senior judge of all, and the head of the judiciary, is the Lord Chancellor:

The law is the true embodiment
Of everything that's excellent.
It has no kind of fault or flaw
And I, my lords, embody the law.
　Gilbert and Sullivan (*Iolanthe*)

His is a curious and unique position: he is a political appointee, given the job by the party in government and therefore losing it if his party loses the election. Usually he is himself a politician, although there is nothing to stop the Prime Minister choosing him from elsewhere.

The Lord Chancellor, currently Lord Irvine of Lairg (a top barrister but not an active politician when appointed), has multiple duties. He is the government's chief spokesman on legal affairs in the House of Lords. He is a member of the Cabinet, and presides in the House of Lords, sitting on the Woolsack in his full-bottomed Speaker's wig. He is a key figure on state ceremonial occasions. He hands the Queen her speech on the opening of Parliament. He is also effectively the Minister of Justice; with the help of a large department he runs the administration of justice and the court system. He is responsible for the appointment of most judges and magistrates, and he advises the Queen or the Prime Minister on whom to appoint to the very highest ranks of the judiciary.

He is also, by virtue of being the Lord Chancellor, a law lord, and can sit on House of Lords appeals. Most Lord Chancellors have been too busy with their many other duties, but a few have made a point of sitting with the law lords as often as possible. Critics argue that the two roles – independent judge and government minister – are incompatible. Lord Irvine's much greater political activity than his predecessors, and his status as a central figure in the Labour administration, have added weight to that argument. His reply is that he would not sit on appeals which might raise a conflict of interests between his political and judicial functions; but that has not been enough to satisfy critics who believe that the two roles should be kept apart and that he should no longer sit as a judge. In 2000 their argument was given a boost by a ruling of the European Court of Human Rights in a case involving the Bailiff – in effect chief minister

## JUDGES

| Called | Court | Referred to as | Title | Addressed in Court | Retiring Age | Salary |
|--------|-------|----------------|-------|--------------------|--------------|--------|
| Lord of Appeal in Ordinary or law lord | House of Lords | Lord Wise | Peerage – Lord Wise | My Lord | 70 | £152,072 |
| Lord Justice of Appeal (appeal court judge) | Court of Appeal | Lord Justice Wise | Knighthood – Sir John (or Dame Jean) Wise | My Lord (or My Lady) | 70 | £144,549 |
| High Court Judge | High Court | Mr (or Mrs) Justice Wise | Knighthood – Sir John (or Dame Jean) Wise | My Lord (or My Lady) | 70 | £127,872 |
| Circuit Judge | Crown Court or county court | His (or Her) Honour Judge Wise QC (if a QC) | None | Your honour* | 70 | £95,873–£103,516 |
| Recorder | Crown Court | Mr (or Mrs) Recorder Wise | None | Your honour | 70 | £436 per day |

*Judges of the Old Bailey, although strictly ordinary circuit judges, are addressed as 'My Lord' (or 'My Lady').

– of Guernsey. He too has several roles, not unlike the Lord Chancellor, and the European Court decided that it was wrong of him to sit as a judge when he had been involved in the passing of the law on which he was to sit in judgment. The Lord Chancellor is not in an identical position, but there is a strong possibility that his judicial role, too, will be challenged.

The top professional judge is the Lord Chief Justice of England and Wales (Scotland and Northern Ireland have their own). Until a few decades ago there was a great deal of political patronage involved in achieving the office: anyone who had been Attorney General had prior claim on the Lord Chief Justice's post. Today it goes with merit. The Lord Chief Justice can sit in any court but, in practice, he mainly presides over the Criminal Division of the Court of Appeal, where he is in a strong position to develop the law in the criminal field and lay down guidelines on sentencing policy, especially on the length of sentences for serious crimes.

The Lord Chief Justice is also the head of the Queen's Bench Division of the High Court and sometimes presides over the Divisional Court there (*see* Chapter II). Lord Woolf is the current holder.

The Master of the Rolls, next in the hierarchy, derives his title from his original duties as the keeper of national records. He sits in the civil branch of the Court of Appeal with two other appeal judges. Like the Lord Chief Justice on the criminal side, the Master of the Rolls has a great deal of influence over the development of the civil law. The judgments of Lord Denning, who held the office for 20 years until retiring in 1982, have profoundly affected many areas of the civil law.

After this, an oddity. The Lords of Appeal in Ordinary – the law lords – sit in the highest court in the land, the House of Lords. But although they are, in judicial terms, junior to the Lord Chief Justice and the Master of the Rolls, they can hear appeals from the decisions of those judges and their courts. The law lords – 12 at present – are the Queen's appointment (on the advice of the Prime Minister, in turn advised by the Lord Chancellor). Two of them are usually Scottish judges; often there is one from Northern Ireland. The others are normally promoted from the Court of Appeal. In addition, present and former Lord Chancellors are eligible to sit. The law lords are created life peers in their own right and, in theory, they are entitled to do everything that any other peer can do. By tradition, however (occasionally broken), they participate only in debates on the law or the administration of justice.

Then come the judges of the Court of Appeal, the 35 Lords Justices who sit regularly in the Civil Division of the court, and some of them also in the Criminal Division. They also sit in the Divisional Court of the Queen's Bench Division. Appeal judges are promoted from the best of the High Court bench. In 1988, for the first time, a woman, Dame Elizabeth Butler-Sloss, was appointed an appeal court judge. Because there had never been one before, there was no precedent for the title she would bear. So, following a statute designed for men, she was, ridiculously, formally referred to as Lord Justice Butler-Sloss, though 'Lady Justice' was allowed in more informal circumstances. In 1999 a second woman was appointed to the appeal court: Dame Brenda Hale.

The next tier down are the High Court judges. In April 2000 there were 102 of them, divided among the three divisions: 69 in the Queen's Bench; 17 in Chancery; and 16 in the Family Division. Judges are normally appointed to the High Court in their early fifties, or some-times even late forties, usually 25 years or more since beginning their legal careers. They are picked almost entirely from the most able of the senior barristers, almost invariably QCs. Solicitors are now eligible for the High Court, though at the time of writing only two have managed to reach that level.

Circuit judges are next in line. There are around 560 of them, serving as judges of the Crown Court hearing serious criminal cases (except the most grave, like murder, which circuit judges can try only by special consent of the senior High Court judge of the court area), or, in the county courts, dealing with lesser civil cases. Unlike High Court judges, they receive no automatic knighthood, their pay is less than a good barrister can earn, and the cases they sit on are usually relatively straightforward. Promotion from the circuit bench to the High Court is no longer rare, but the vast majority of lawyers appointed to the post know that they are likely to remain there until reaching the pensionable age of 72 (or 70 if they were appointed after March 1995). Circuit judges tend to come mainly from the middle ranks of senior barristers and from successful solicitors (who form about 13 per cent of the 560 or so circuit judges). The real high-fliers, the most successful barristers, would hope to be invited on to the High Court bench and would not normally be interested in becoming circuit judges, for reasons of both finance and prestige. Most of those who do apply to be interviewed for the circuit bench are perfectly competent barristers who accept that they are not quite of High Court calibre and that they can get no further at the Bar. They plump for security and a pension. It is a source of concern, however, to the judiciary and the legal profession that, with such a large number of circuit judges needed, too many of them may not be of sufficiently high quality.

The lowest tier of full-time judges, district judges (formerly known as registrars), deal with many preliminary matters before trial, and play an important role in the courts dealing with divorce. They are the filters through which all divorce applications pass, and they make most of the decisions about money and property following divorce. District judges, of whom there are around 400, also act as judges in small claims arbitrations, involving up to £5000.

The lowest judicial level is part-time. There are more than 1,350 recorders, mostly barristers. They sit for 20 or so days a year in the Crown Court and county court. Appointment as a recorder gives a practising lawyer a taste of judging which he may later try to turn into a full-time occupation. It also gives the Lord Chancellor the opportunity to assess whether he has the ability to become a circuit or even a High Court judge. In the county courts there are some 750 deputy district judges. Often, senior barristers may be asked to hear cases as deputy High Court judges.

## How they are chosen

Until 1998, becoming a High Court judge was by invitation only and it was the Lord Chancellor who did the inviting. It was considered the height of bad form to mention an interest in the job. Now, vacancies are advertised but, in practice, not much has changed. The Lord Chancellor chooses from a small and limited pool made up almost entirely of senior barristers – though the door is open to allow the possibility of solicitors becoming High Court judges. The first former solicitor to have come through that opening, Mr Justice Sachs, was appointed in 1993. The second, in 2000, was the first to be appointed directly from private practice.

In former days, when the Bar was small, the Lord Chancellor knew all the able QCs personally and could assess which of them were good judge material. It is much more difficult now. He cannot know everyone; he has to base his appointments on advice from other judges, senior lawyers and representatives of organizations that have close contacts with potential candidates (like the chairman of the Bar, and president of the Law Society), as well as reports from his departmental officials. Up to 1900 people may be asked for their opinion, the Lord Chancellor told the House of Commons Home Affairs committee in 1999. Potential judges are graded for qualities such as humanity, courtesy and their understanding of people and society, as well as more obvious legal attributes. The system was unrivalled in its breadth and its thoroughness, he said. But there's also an informal side to the Lord Chancellor's trawl. A judge who has been particularly impressed (or the opposite) with the performance of a barrister who has appeared before him might tell the Lord Chancellor so. Reputations spread, but also negative rumours get around. Little by little a dossier is built up. There will also be information about barristers from occasions when they have applied for lesser appointments, to become QCs or part-time judges, for instance. All this information is stored in the Lord Chancellor's department (as are data on potential solicitor judges). So by the time a senior barrister comes to be considered for the High Court bench, the Lord Chancellor has quite a lot of information on him which he can supplement by further inquiries from anyone who knows the candidate. And candidates for the High Court bench will have done stints as part-time judges, so their judicial ability is not entirely unknown.

In a small, but growing, number of instances, High Court judges have been appointed after a stint as full-time circuit judges rather than straight from the Bar. That allows those who were not originally thought of as high-fliers to prove themselves at the lower level of the judiciary.

The final decision is taken by the Lord Chancellor after discussion with his senior judges. Such a system does, however, throw up some strange decisions. Some of the most brilliant barristers have never been offered high judicial appointment (for reasons which are never made public though they may have something to do with their personal life rather than their legal ability). At the same time there are some High Court judges of lesser ability. In particular, it is claimed that the way judges are chosen leads to a perpetuation of the male stranglehold. There have been only two women appeal court judges; in 2000 there were only nine women High Court judges out of 102; and women make up only around eight per cent of circuit judges.

The argument against the present system is that the informal chats and soundings about potential candidates tend to take place among senior judges and lawyers who are male; they would know male colleagues rather better than females, partly because women, especially those with families, don't go to as many legal functions and don't spend as much time socializing at the Inns of Court, or networking in influential legal circles.

The Lord Chancellor, Lord Irvine, like his predecessor, denies any suggestion of bias or discrimination against women or ethnic minorities. 'The beauty of this system is that it is so wide-ranging across so many people that the risk of prejudice or discrimination . . . is reduced.' He insists that merit is the only criterion for appointment, and argues that the only reason there are so few women in the judiciary is that women of the necessary age and experience to become judges are still in a small minority. As more women reach the upper reaches of the legal profession, more will be in the pool from which judges are chosen, and more women will become judges.

An identical argument is used to meet the criticism that too few lawyers from the ethnic minorities are on the bench – none at High Court level or above; only six out of 560 circuit judges, 31 out of more than 1,300 part-time recorders.

The Lord Chancellor urges more women and lawyers from the minorities to apply for judicial posts, but is adamant that there should be nothing that smacks of positive discrimination.

On the secrecy of the appointments procedure, the Lord Chancellor says that he has to preserve the confidentiality of other people's comments about potential candidates; otherwise people advising him would not be free with their remarks or opinions. But critics find it unacceptable that candidates might be denied a judgeship because of something – which might be totally incorrect – said in secret by an unidentified source.

Dissatisfaction with the existing system is widespread and growing. The Law Society, which represents solicitors, went as far as refusing to participate in the process because of its annoyance at what it saw as 'secret soundings' which were still highly biased in favour of barristers.

Calls for reform of the appointments system have come from many quarters. The civil liberties organization Justice, for instance, is among many bodies to propose some kind of judicial appointments commission, made up of both lawyer and non-lawyer members, to advise the Lord Chancellor about candidates; it also calls for the appointments procedure to be transparent and more open to public scrutiny. The Lord Chancellor, however, has adamantly rejected these ideas. He yielded to pressure to an extent, by appointing Sir Leonard Peach, the former Commissioner for Public Appointments, to look into the appointments system, but made it clear that Sir Leonard's terms of reference barred him from proposing a judicial appointments commission. Sir Leonard had to be satisfied with recommending a watchdog to oversee the appointments process.

Few critics, however, want to go as far as the American system of a public hearing for the appointment of senior judges, especially in the light of the televised fiasco of Justice Clarence Thomas's ordeal over his nomination to the Supreme Court.

Occasionally, but increasingly in the 1990s, barristers who have been sounded out to become judges decline the honour. The reason is often financial. A very successful QC, especially one who does commercial work, would be earning at least £500,000 a year and possibly nearer £1 million. (At the top level, around 20 QCs are estimated to earn in excess of £1 million a year.) To give up that sort of money for the prestige of becoming a judge for a salary little more than £100,000 has proved too great a sacrifice for a number of high-quality barristers.

Some high-fliers at the Bar prefer to widen their horizons rather than join the strait-jacketed judicial hierarchy. They take on prestigious jobs in the City's financial institutions, or become the heads of Oxbridge colleges. Other top QCs prefer to remain at the Bar because they find the work more interesting than that of a High Court judge and are put off by some of the more tiresome duties judges are asked to perform, like going on circuit – being absent from home for weeks on end hearing criminal trials in provincial towns and cities. The job of a High Court judge can often be repetitive and unstimulating; the carrot is the possibility of rising higher.

Promotion to the Court of Appeal, and then to the House of Lords, is, in theory, in the Queen's gift and given on recommendation by the Prime Minister, but, in practice, these appointments follow the Lord Chancellor's advice. Once a judge has already been on the bench it is of course a far easier job to evaluate his ability for the highest judicial posts.

The junior judicial appointments (circuit judge, district judge, recorder) are all advertised. Any reasonably senior barrister (not necessarily a QC) or solicitor can apply to the Lord Chancellor, and applicants are interviewed and assessed just as they would be for a job anywhere else. An applicant for a full-time appointment will need to have served several years as a recorder.

There is some support in principle for another method of expanding the pool from which judges are chosen. Legal academics – professors and teachers of law – are often among the most knowledgeable experts in the country in their fields. It is true that they lack the relevant expertise to conduct full-scale trials with witnesses and, for this reason, there are few who argue that they should be appointed to the High Court. But they would be entirely suitable in the Court of Appeal or the House of Lords. Argument on fine points of law precisely suits their training and experience.

Most countries have some form of career structure for judges but there is virtually no support for introducing a career judiciary in England. In France, for example, a young lawyer can choose, while still in his twenties, to become a judge. He will be specially trained for it and start at the bottom with perhaps a minor post in a small town. In time he will expect to work his way up the ladder, just as in most other career structures.

English judges and lawyers believe that our system works reasonably well and throws up judges of high quality and undoubted integrity. They argue that a career judiciary, and the jostling for advancement or particular postings that it would involve, would render judges more susceptible to state or other outside interference or persuasion. Whether or not that is true, it would require a revolution in the legal system to change so drastically our mode of picking judges. There are no signs of either a need or a demand for such a wholesale change.

## Who are they?

Up to 40 or so years ago, it was difficult even to consider becoming a barrister without some private funds or financial backing. Few grants were available from public funds to study law and it was much harder to make a living in the first few years of practice. A barrister often had to be supported financially, not only for his period of study but perhaps for two or three years after being called to the Bar. So the judges that emerged out of those barristers tended to come from a narrow background.

The great legal aid explosion of the 1960s changed that and made it possible for young barristers to start earning very near the beginning of their careers; and the availability of local authority grants allowed more aspiring barristers to pursue their studies. The pool from which the judiciary was chosen became socially wider.

Most of our judges, however, are still the products of the generation of barristers who, on the whole, had some source of private funds in their early years. Not surprisingly, the majority came from the comfortable middle and upper-middle classes, though there were some notable exceptions – Lord Denning's father was a draper.

It follows, too, that most of our present crop of judges, coming from relatively affluent families, have gone to public school and then to Oxford or Cambridge – more than 80 per cent of the senior judiciary. It is a proportion which has been approximately the same for the entire post-war period. There is a sprinkling of grammar schoolboys who went to Oxbridge because they were clever and got scholarships; and some public schoolboys who went to universities other than Oxbridge. One recent Court of Appeal judge was educated at a Welsh grammar school and didn't go to university; Dame Elizabeth Butler-Sloss, the most senior woman judge in the country, also decided against university; a current appeal court judge's father was a publican. They are very much the exceptions.

So the picture of our typical English judge emerges: middle class or above, public school, Oxbridge. Traditionally, judges have tended to be politically conservative, but that is changing. There is even a highly respected appeal judge (Lord Justice Sedley) who was once a member of the Communist party, and more judges today than ever before would vote Labour. But psychologists might say that young people who go into law are showing a leaning towards things that are certain and slow to change, and a liking for the framework of rules. They would be supporters of the status quo, rather than radicals out to change it. Their careers as barristers would reinforce those predilections.

Most barristers who become judges – certainly those in London – have already spent 25 or even more years working, and often eating and drinking, in the rarefied and somewhat artificial atmosphere of the Inns of Court, with their obscure and ancient customs and traditions. When they become judges the cocoon is tightened around them. The dignity of their office and the importance of being seen to be impartial and uncontroversial often demand that they distance themselves from their former habits and haunts. The result can be an increasing remoteness from the mainstream of society. The longer they serve as judges, the more they may appear to be out of touch with the problems of the ordinary person. The charge is made against them that they live in an ivory tower, remote from the vicissitudes of most people's daily lives, unable from their lofty heights to appreciate the difficulties that lesser humans face.

In 1999 a large public attitudes survey by Hazel Genn of University College London found that a large proportion of those asked had a negative, but poorly informed, image of the judiciary: 'They sound like a bunch of pompous old weirdos. They're all old men . . .'; '. . . fuddy old judge. He might have lived in the real world 40 years ago, but now

71

he is living in a mansion in the middle of Berkshire . . . They are not in touch with reality'; 'My stereotype comes from the telly and they're always portrayed as 70 plus, wrinkly, upper class fellows.'

Such widespread attitudes are not good news for a judiciary trying hard to shed what judges see as a totally unfair, long out-of-date view of what they are like today.

There is no doubt that in the past many judges believed themselves to be above the common herd. They were treated like royalty, especially when travelling round the country to sit in the peripatetic assize courts (a system now replaced by the permanent crown courts), and it is scarcely surprising that many of them started believing that they were akin to royalty. But things have changed. Judges today are convinced that they no longer inhabit that judicial ivory tower.

The generation of judges who, rightly or wrongly, were tarred with the image of out-of-touch remoteness and arrogance have largely retired from the bench. Very few dinosaurs, if any, remain. The new judicial generation consists of people who live more or less normal lives. Of course many of them will be better off than most (though very few these days have the kind of private incomes that many in the past were accustomed to), but that does not mean that they are out of touch. They take public transport, wheel trolleys around supermarkets, sink pints at their local, do the washing up, watch television and have rebellious children who play loud music. The two most senior judges, the Lord Chief Justice and the Master of the Rolls, are thoroughly modern men, untainted by pomposity or any feeling of superiority; and most recently appointed judges are very far indeed from the caricatures the public has become used to. The image of the judiciary which the public still has seems to stem largely, as Professor Genn's research bears out, from inaccurate television dramas and reading about untypical but highly publicized judicial gaffes in the newspapers.

The main valid criticism about today's judiciary is not so much that the judges on the bench are full of out-of-date attitudes, but that too many of them are male and white.

There is a limit, though, to how much judges should be just like anyone else. The English system of justice depends on respect for the judiciary, its independence and its integrity. To some extent that requires the judge to be a slightly awesome figure on a pedestal, and not one of the people. He must be Caesar's wife, above suspicion, careful and restrained in what he does and says.

It is also essential to the reputation of judges for impartiality that they have no financial or personal interests that might be thought to affect the way they considered or decided a case they were hearing. Very few critics have ever suggested that British judges are actually biased – but they must also not give the perception of bias.

In 1998, Lord Hoffmann, one of the five law lords hearing the case of General Pinochet, the former Chilean dictator wanted in Spain for various atrocities, failed to disclose a link with one of the parties in the case. He was director of a charity run by the human rights campaigning body Amnesty International, which was represented at the appeal, arguing strongly against giving Pinochet immunity from prosecution. When Lord Hoffmann's undisclosed link was eventually made public, the law lords' decision was nullified and the case had to be heard all over again.

The debate sparked by the Hoffmann affair focused on the need for judges to be more open about possible conflicts of interests – not just obvious ones like holding shares in a company involved in a case before them, or being friends with one of the parties, but membership of particular societies, like the Freemasons, or having strong views on controversial issues, like hunting. There were calls for a judges' register, like the one in which MPs list their relevant links.

In 1999 the Court of Appeal heard five separate appeals raising issues of possible bias by judges. The court laid down that judges should admit direct links pertinent to the case, like knowing a witness, but not that they were gay or Freemasons, or their religion or their opinions. But in one of the appeals, they ordered a retrial, because the part-time judge had written and spoken extensively in terms which were critical of defendants – insurance companies – in personal injury cases; he might be thought to be less than impartial when he himself tried such cases.

# The role of the judge

The judge is a crucial figure in the English trial system, more so than in other countries. In the English process the result of a case turns very largely on what happens during the trial itself. In most other legal systems, much of the vital work is done before trial. There is much more documentary background material, and in a criminal case there has been a thorough investigation of the crime and the suspect long before an accused has to step into the dock.

The judge in an English trial plays many parts. First, he supervises the conduct of the trial. It is up to the parties and their lawyers to present their case, whether civil or criminal, but it is the judge who has to make sure that the rules are kept and that the trial flows as it should. A judge is like a football referee – if he is too lax, never blowing his whistle, the game gets out of control, the players take liberties and an unjust result may follow. If he is too strict and blows the whistle too often the game is ossified and the players get no chance to show their paces and use their skills; the game is equally distorted. A judge must put his firm stamp on the trial without taking over the proceedings.

Second, he is the sole arbiter of any legal issues that arise during the trial, in particular about the admissibility of evidence. This is especially important in criminal trials, where the case can hang on whether certain evidence can be put to the jury or not. There are numbers of other legal decisions which may need to be made in the course of a trial and which will affect it significantly.

Third, in civil cases the judge himself has to decide the result. Apart from infrequent libel cases and even rarer claims for false imprisonment, slander and malicious prosecution, juries have disappeared from civil trials. The judge is the sole arbiter. He not only determines who wins and who loses but also such issues as what damages to award, how to distribute money or property, how to settle disputes over the children of broken marriages, how an ambiguous rule should be interpreted, and so on through a wide range of decisions.

Fourth, when giving his judgment in a civil trial he has to interpret and clarify the law when there are gaps in it, or where it is unclear or ambiguous. Some would say that judges go further and actually make new law.

Fifth, in a criminal trial the judge has the important task of summing up to the jury. The verdict is the sole province of the jury, but it is the judge's duty both to guide them on the law and to summarize impartially the main factual points given by witnesses in evidence. Cases have been won or lost on a judge's summing-up. It has been known for a judge skilfully to nudge a jury towards his own conclusion, whether for conviction or acquittal. But this has to be done subtly. Juries resent being told what verdict to reach, and a crude summing-up may well be counter-productive.

Finally, a judge has to pass sentence on defendants who have pleaded guilty or who have been convicted by a jury. He is confined to the limits laid down by the law and within those limits there is often an unwritten informal tariff for particular kinds of offences. Judges also have guidance from the Court of Appeal about levels of sentencing. Nevertheless, sentencing is an awesome responsibility, especially where the decision is whether or not to send an offender to prison.

## Training

With all these different and difficult functions to perform it would be logical to assume that some intensive training is given to judges before they are let loose in the courts. Not so.

It is one of the quirks of the system that a senior judge, once appointed, may be allocated to an area of the law about which he knows very little, and on which he gets only a modicum of training or guidance. It's not uncommon for a barrister who has spent his entire professional career doing civil work to be called on to try serious criminal cases, or for someone whose practice was mainly in the criminal courts to have to decide family disputes. There is an unspoken, perhaps arrogant, assumption that anyone good enough to be appointed to the bench has the ability to turn his hand to any branch of the law. In practice the results of our rather haphazard system are mixed. Many a judge becomes known for his mastery of a field that he hardly touched as a barrister, but there are others who only feel at ease in the speciality they developed at the Bar.

Until the 1960s the concept of giving judges any training to help them fulfil their new and perhaps unfamiliar duties was considered an insult to barristers. Not until 1963 was the first tentative step taken in the form of a one-day non-compulsory conference on sentencing. Judicial training (or judicial studies, as judges prefer to describe it) has greatly expanded since then and it has become more formalized with the setting up of a Judicial Studies Board to run courses.

In 1972 a committee of the law reform body Justice recommended that there should be a three- to six-month training period for all judges on their appointment. In 1978 an inter-departmental government committee suggested a period of one or two weeks, depending on whether the new appointee had experience in the criminal courts or not.

The present system is close to that modest proposal in terms of training time. There are two main kinds of residential course: one is for beginners, mainly newly appointed recorders; and the other a refresher course for more experienced circuit judges. The novices' course lasts four days. They are given lectures by experienced judges about the duties they have to carry out in court, how to conduct a trial and the problems they may encounter. The main focus is on sentencing. They attend lectures by probation officers, social workers, prison officials, psychiatrists and penologists, as well as senior judges. These are designed to give trainee judges an idea of the interaction between offenders, their crimes and the options available to treat or punish them. They are fed with the latest important Court of Appeal decisions, prison statistics and information about trends in imprisonment and the alternatives to prison, like community service. They will all at some stage visit a prison and a young offender institution.

Perhaps the most effective parts of the course are the sentencing exercises. The participants are given an outline of a crime committed, and information about the offender's history and background – the same information as judges in real trials would have. The facts are based on cases which have been before the Court of Appeal. The trainee judges discuss the cases among themselves, in small panels, and decide on the sentences they would pass. Their results are analysed and discussed by experienced judges and compared to the sentences the Court of Appeal imposed when it dealt with the real cases.

The refresher course for more experienced judges lasts for four days (regularly repeated for every judge) but is more advanced. The judges are assumed to know the basic principles, but they, too, have to be kept up to date with the latest case-law, and trends in sentencing policy and penology. There is much more discussion among themselves, and with senior judges, on issues actually confronting them in the courts, and fewer formal lectures. Sentencing is still likely to be the focus.

There are also residential induction courses for judges in the civil courts, and an increasing number of shorter update seminars, as well as courses on specific topics. For instance, judges who have responsibility for making decisions under the Children Act will all have had to attend special courses on the subject. All judges will have been given a course on how to deal with the Human Rights Act, coming into force in October 2000, incorporating the European Convention on Human Rights and likely to lead to a new range of cases coming before the courts.

But even with these improvements, is the training provided any-where near enough? Good advocates do not necessarily make good judges. The skills required of the two disciplines are not identical. Yet our system requires the transition from barrister (or solicitor) to judge to be made with only minimal training, though admittedly there is a period of part-time judicial work to ease the passage into full-time judging. But even the newest recorders can send people to prison after a few days' training.

# The judge as lawmaker

Judges, according to the traditional litany, do not make law, they only interpret existing law; they decide what the law already is. It is Parliament's role to create new law, not the judiciary's. That may be a perfectly reasonable theoretical position to hold and it is in keeping with the constitutional division between the judiciary and the legislature. It does not, however, conform to the facts. It is in the nature of the UK system of law that judges can and do make law.

Most countries in the world have legal codes. Every branch of the law is governed by a code which lays down exactly what can and cannot be done. It tries to cater for every contingency. When there is a problem the judges turn to the code to see what it says. Of course there are some gaps and some ambiguities, and judges have to resolve these, but their role is secondary.

Britain has no such comprehensive codes, and finding out what the law is can be rather more complicated. There are two main sources of law and the judges play a central role in both. The first is statute law: acts of Parliament (from which may stem a whole range of secondary legislation and lesser laws passed by other bodies, such as local authorities). The United Kingdom Parliament is sovereign; it can pass any law on any topic – though subject to the paramountcy of European Community law. But many of these laws are imperfectly drafted. They are not always clear. The intention behind them can be obscure. There are gaps, both deliberate and accidental. Sometimes two interpretations are possible. When there is room for doubt about what an act of Parliament actually means, it is the judges' job to clarify it. Their interpretation can have the most dramatic results, not just for the people involved in the case itself but for millions of other people in a similar position.

The common law of England, the other main source of law, will not be found in any act of Parliament. It has developed over the centuries through the decisions of judges in particular cases that have come before them, in areas where there is no statute. These decisions are not taken haphazardly – the law would be chaotic and uncertain if it were left entirely to each judge to decide the case according to his whim. So there has grown up the doctrine of precedent, based on the understandable assumption that the higher courts, made up of the most senior judges, know better than the lower judiciary. There are courts whose decisions must be followed by lower ranking courts. Decisions of the House of Lords, the highest court, are binding on all the other courts below it, and even on itself unless the law lords are convinced that their own previous decision was wrong. If the House of Lords has not ruled on a particular point, then it is the Court of Appeal's decisions that are binding on the lower courts. A High Court judge, for instance, must follow them, even if he thinks they are wrong.

What can a judge do if the precedent he is bound to follow achieves injustice? A former law lord put it this way:

Justice that pays no regard to precedent can be positively injustice. Precedents can be grossly irritating and confining when they exist and prevent you from going the way you would prefer to go. But I do not agree that justice can always be arrived at by ignoring precedent. If you are not bound, of course, it's another matter. Do the just thing as you see it. But sometimes that is quite impossible.

I would struggle might and main to differentiate between a line of existing cases and the instant case in order to arrive at a just conclusion. But if there is really no substantial difference between the case I have in hand and earlier cases I cannot, consistent with my duty, forget those earlier cases, although I might be most unhappy in coming to the conclusion I find myself driven to arrive at. And leave it to Parliament. Because I think that if you do not adopt that approach, chaos can arrive, and chaos and justice in my view are ill neighbours.

Lord Denning, who retired as Master of the Rolls in 1982, argued passionately that judges were too conservative in interpreting the law to achieve the just result. His philosophy is summed up in his book *The Discipline of Law* (Butterworths, 1979):

Let it not be thought from this discourse that I am against the doctrine of precedent. I am not. All that I am against is its too rigid application, a rigidity which insists that a bad precedent must necessarily be followed. I would treat

79

it as you would a path through the woods: you must follow it certainly so as to reach your end, but you must not let the path become too overgrown, you must cut out the dead wood and trim off the side branches, else you will find yourself lost in thickets and brambles. My plea is simply to keep the path of justice clear of obstructions which would impede it.

Lord Denning's scant regard for precedents which stood in the way of what he believed to be justice attracted much criticism from many of his legal and judicial colleagues. A goodly proportion of his decisions in the Court of Appeal were overturned by the House of Lords. But his insistence on doing justice even by straining the law also gained him respect and admiration from millions of people outside the legal world.

But did he take the function of a judge too far? The late Lord Devlin, one of the top legal minds of recent times, was one of the main proponents of judicial conservatism. Judges, he argued in *The Judge* (OUP, 1979), are not fitted for a creative, dynamic law-making role, nor is it desirable that they should be in the forefront of making law. Nor should they become social reformers, or become professionally concerned with social justice:

It might be dangerous if they were. They might not administer the law fairly if they were constantly questioning its justice or agitating their minds about its improvement.

But if judges should not see themselves as social reformers, they must inevitably be aware of the social and possibly the political background of the cases that come before them. Judges too have private opinions and prejudices. John Griffith suggests, in *The Politics of the Judiciary* (Fontana, 1997), that the higher judiciary

... have by their education and training and the pursuit of their profession as barristers, acquired a strikingly homogeneous collection of attitudes, beliefs and principles, which to them represents the public interest. They do not always express it as such. But it is the lodestar by which they navigate.

In theory, judges must try to put aside not only their own views but also what they know or suspect might be the wider practical consequences of their decisions. Professor Griffith doesn't believe that complete neutrality can be achieved in practice. Judges, he argues, by their own inclinations and because of the status of the judiciary as part of the authority within the state, will tend to make conservative decisions which usually support the existing order as they see it.

Judges vigorously deny that they come to decisions on the basis of political considerations. In any event, they argue, is it not in the public interest that judges should be conservative, favour the status quo, and be suspicious of flash new legal theories and arguments based on a particular view of social justice? Lord Devlin wrote:

Law is the gatekeeper of the status quo. There is always a host of new ideas galloping around the outskirts of a society's thought. All of them seek admission but each must first win its spurs; the law at first resists, but will submit to a conqueror and become his servant. (*The Judge*)

The debate continues, but it has taken a new turn. There is no doubt that judges have become more obviously aware of the social, political and economic circumstances that form the backdrop to any case before them, and the practical consequences of reaching a particular decision. They are also much more conscious of public opinion on particular issues and, although they must not formulate their decisions to conform to public opinion, it can, judges admit, have some effect on their minds. Judges are perhaps more adventurous than they used to be, not as awed by precedent or as timid in making known their views on the law. These adventurous judicial attitudes have become most evident in the robust way in which High Court judges have treated applications for judicial review. It is difficult to discern in their decisions – many of them highly critical of government policy – any dominant philosophy of conservatism or reluctance to challenge the law's rigidity. Indeed, the enthusiasm with which many judges have extended the bounds of judicial review suggests that we are passing through one of the most radical, activist phases of judicial thinking for many decades, a feeling confirmed by some recent appointments to the highest court, the House of Lords.

At the same time Parliament is becoming far more active in passing new laws. The sheer amount of legislation pouring through Westminster is having its effect on the courts. Statute law is coming to dominate the common law. But far from the judges' influence becoming less as a result, the volume and, often, the inadequacy of modern legislation are ensuring that the role of judges in interpreting the law is becoming more essential and their ability to mould the law – whether for good or bad – is now greater than it has been for many decades.

Now there is the Human Rights Act, which will undoubtedly enhance further all these trends towards greater judicial intervention. When it comes into force in October 2000, and the European Convention on Human Rights becomes part of English law, the judges are going to have to make decisions over a whole range of issues with political, personal and social consequences, affecting the family, freedom of speech, immigration, the right to privacy, health, the right to die, and many other interests. The claim that judges don't make the law, and don't meddle in politics or in society's social fabric, will become even more impossible to argue.

CHAPTER V
# The Magistrates

If the English system of criminal justice had to depend on our professional judges, it would break down immediately. There are just too few judges to cope. It doesn't collapse because the judiciary is backed by more than 30,000 magistrates who, astonishingly, are unpaid, part-time and amateur. The magistrates (or justices of the peace, or JPs) are not just important cogs: they are the mainstay of the criminal justice system. They deal with more than 95 per cent of all criminal cases. Around two million people pass through their courts every year. Admittedly, most of them are charged with trivial crimes, for instance minor traffic offences, but in 1998 48,000 adult offenders were sent to prison by magistrates.

This great power over the lives of others is concentrated in the hands of people who are chosen in secret, are given little training to enable them to do their job, and work on a voluntary basis. Certainly if a legal system were to be created from scratch, no one would think of giving work of such importance to non-professionals. Like so many other English institutions, the lay magistracy grew and developed over the centuries until it became so vital a part of our legal system that it is now inconceivable to think seriously of changing it in any fundamental way.

The first Justices or Keepers of the Peace were appointed as early as 1195 by Richard I, the Lionheart, and for the next century and a half they acted as a sort of primitive police force. During the fourteenth century, and especially during the economic and social chaos that followed the Black Death, they became in effect the local government, and they were also given the powers to dispense summary justice. A statute of 1361 provides:

In every county of England shall be assigned for the keeping of the peace one lord and with him three or four of the most worthy in the county, with some learned in the law, and they shall have the power to restrain the offenders . . . and to pursue, arrest, take and chastise them according to their trespass and offence.

They kept all their roles for five centuries, though the distinction between their policing and judicial functions was not always clearly defined. During the great reform movements of the mid-nineteenth century they lost first their police role to the embryo modern police force, and then their administrative role to the emerging local councils, but they retained their judicial duties.

In London, the lay magistracy went through a period of great, and justified, unpopularity during the eighteenth century. Magistrates had a financial stake in the booty found on captured criminals. They were corrupt. Justice could be bought. So appalling had the reputation and standing of London's 'poor courts' become that the government passed a law allowing the appointment of lawyers as full-time stipendiary (paid) magistrates. Henry Fielding, the author of *Tom Jones*, was among the first of these stipendiaries, who worked in a house in Bow Street, forerunner of the famous Bow Street Magistrates' Court, the senior magistrates' court in the country. Fielding was succeeded by his brother, the blind John Fielding, whose Bow Street Runners were the direct precursors of today's Metropolitan Police Force.

The introduction of the few stipendiaries made little inroad into the system of lay justices, which eventually recovered its reputation and continued to expand. It was not until the 1920s and 1930s, however, when motoring offences started to bring the articulate middle classes into the justices' courts, that reforms began to be made which laid the foundations of the modern magistrates' courts. The system, as it exists today, is the result of a post-war reform following the recommendations of a Royal Commission in 1948.

# How are they chosen?

A magistrate need have no formal qualifications. But there are some disqualifications – those not eligible include bankrupts, people with convictions for serious crime, members of the armed forces, the police and various others working in the criminal justice system. Spouses or partners of most of those categories would also be ineligible. So would anyone with a serious infirmity or disability – but blind JPs are acceptable, though they don't sit on cases requiring the inspection of documents or, for instance, watching CCTV footage of a crime. Members of Parliament, parliamentary candidates or full-time election agents cannot be JPs in their own constituencies, though they can sit in others. 'Any person whose office or whose work would conflict or be incompatible with the duties of a magistrate' cannot be one, nor can close relatives of justices on the same bench.

The positive virtues magistrates need to have are vague. The guidance notes for new applicants lists 'six key qualities': good character, understanding and communication, social awareness, maturity and sound temperament, sound judgement, commitment and reliability. An official booklet puts it this way:

The first and much the most important consideration in selecting justices of the peace is that they should be personally suitable in character, integrity and understanding for the important work which they have to perform, and that they should be generally recognized as such by those among whom they live and work. Under no circumstances will the Lord Chancellor appoint anyone as a reward for past services of any kind.

Around 1600 magistrates are appointed every year. Until recently, the process of choosing them was even more secretive than it is today, giving rise to the criticism that the magistracy was a self-perpetuating oligarchy of local worthies. The system is now more open, with the aim of trawling as wide a pool of candidates as possible. Constitutionally, the appointment of magistrates lies with the Lord Chancellor, but in practice the task of choosing suitable candidates has been given to advisory committees all around the country. These committees recommend names to the Lord Chancellor (or, in Lancashire, the Chancellor of the Duchy of Lancaster), who then formally appoints them. He has the power to reject the committee's recommendation or to appoint someone without their advice, but he rarely does either. The Lord Chancellor relies heavily on the advisory committees, who have the local knowledge and the opportunity to assess and interview those they think might have the qualities to sit on the bench.

There are over 100 advisory committees in England and Wales, each with responsibility for a specified area. Until 1992, their members' names were not revealed, thus reinforcing the image of a tightly knit group of like-minded people who recommended people just like themselves. It is far more open now. The names of all committee members must be open to public inspection, as well as the name and address of the committee's secretary, so that people wanting to put forward a name know to whom to write.

The advisory committees generally consist of about 12 members. It is a rule that a committee should include at least one member from each of the main political parties and some members who are politically independent. The aim, according to the guidance booklet, is that membership of the advisory committees should be 'widely spread through the area covered and drawn from different walks of life'. The Lord Chancellor appoints people to the committee whom he believes are in touch with local affairs, active and established in the local community, and therefore in a good position to assess who would make a good JP. At least one-third of an advisory committee's members should not be magistrates.

Anyone is entitled to recommend anyone else to the advisory committee as a suitable candidate for the magistracy. But a person can put himself forward, something which is greatly encouraged. The trouble is that most people don't realize that they don't have to wait to be asked, or they lack the confidence to suggest themselves as suitable. So the majority of candidates are approached by the committee because they are known personally or by reputation to committee members. There is nothing wrong with this provided the advisory committees themselves are drawn from a wide social range, an aim which is being pursued, for instance, by making sure that one out of three on each committee is not a JP.

But there is still some criticism that advisory committees, being largely middle and upper class and 'establishment', tend to choose as magistrates others of their kind, and that the advisory committee system therefore produces a largely self-perpetuating oligarchy from which, in general, the ethnic minorities and working-class people are excluded. In an extreme example, a 1973 survey of Rochdale magistrates showed that 29 out of the 43 were Freemasons or members of the Rotary Club and that not a single one was Roman Catholic. Even then such an imbalance was untypical. Today it would certainly be contrary to the Lord Chancellor's department's policy – a 'jobs for the boys' approach would be severely frowned on officially. But it may be to some extent inevitable under the present selection system. As recently as 1994 a survey revealed that Conservatives far outnumbered Labour supporters in the magistracy, even in areas where Labour voters dominated at election time. That finding would be even more marked following the 1997 general election.

Until 1998 the government's official aim was to try to achieve a balance in the magistracy between the two main political parties. But this has proved impossible and unrealistic, and the policy now is to achieve a social balance, taking into account socio-economic factors. This, the government now believes, should make the magistracy more representative of the community it serves.

## Who are they?

Sir Thomas Skyrme, the most eminent historian of the magistracy, claims:

The system of lay justices reflects, through citizen participation, the traditional English involvement of the layman in the administration of justice. It enables the citizen to see that the law is his law, administered by men and women like himself, and that it is not the esoteric preserve of the lawyers.

(*The Changing Image of the Magistracy*)

87

But the vast majority of magistrates – one study put it as high as 84 per cent – belong to what would loosely be called the professional or managerial classes – in other words, the middle classes and above. Only 16 per cent come from the skilled or semi-skilled working class and trades union officials. The Lord Chancellor's department admits that one of the reasons there are not more working-class magistrates is because they don't come to the attention of the advisory committees in the same way as middle-class candidates do – they don't move in the same circles or belong to the same clubs. Those that become active in politics or trades union affairs might be recommended by their party or union officials, but others may just never have their ability noticed and brought to the attention of the advisory committee. The hope is that, as the appointments system is opened up and the membership of the advisory committees is widened, a greater range of candidates will come to the surface.

In recent years, the Lord Chancellor's department, in an attempt to increase the social base of the magistracy, has taken to advertising for suitable candidates in the popular media, including tabloid newspapers. One of the campaigns was specifically aimed at showing that people from unlikely jobs and trades – taxi-drivers, aerobics teachers, couriers – could become magistrates.

There are other reasons for the social imbalance. Working-class people are often loath to allow their names to be put forward, either through lack of interest or because they fear that their job or promotion prospects might be endangered by their absences from work; or even on the ground that becoming a JP would cause tensions with their workmates and colleagues. These factors are exacerbated during a period of recession and high unemployment. If a working JP loses his job, he might find it difficult to get another once a prospective employer finds out he has to have a day off every fortnight. (JPs have to sit at least 26 half-days a year, but preferably 35 half-days). This is not confined to working-class wage-earners. An applicant for the headmastership of a school was told that he could have the job on condition that he gave up his magisterial duties. Working magistrates may also have to sacrifice part of their earnings. There is no financial reward for being on the bench, only expenses and a limited loss of earnings allowance – usually not enough to compensate for money lost.

There should be no difficulty, in theory, about absences from work. Under the law, employers cannot object to their workers' taking time off to sit on the bench. In practice, however, there are many subtle ways in which an employer can make his displeasure known and discourage prospective JPs.

Whatever the reasons for the social imbalance, it has led to comments that there is too much of a gap between the mainly middle-class, white, comfortably off magistrates and the typical defendants who appear before them. Magistrates, it is suggested, cannot really understand the problems, nor the culture, of the kind of people they try. If true, this would contradict one of the aims of the system of lay justices.

More recently, concern has been expressed about the low proportion of magistrates from the ethnic minorities, especially West Indian, Indian and Pakistani. The latest figures show that around four per cent are black or Asian, but in recent years the proportion has risen. In 1998 more than six per cent of JPs appointed were from the ethnic minorities. They tend to sit in the larger urban centres with a significant proportion of minorities.

The attempt to get more women on the bench has been more successful, partly because many more women than men, even today, are not in full-time work. Women now make up around 49 per cent of magistrates, just below 15,000.

A fine balance has to be drawn. It is crucial to our system of justice to have magistrates who are good at what they do. But it is equally important for the public at large, as well as for defendants in particular, to feel that they are not too remote from those who sit in judgment on them. If it were widely thought that magistrates were too unrepresentative of the society they served, their reputation would suffer and public respect for our system of justice would be damaged.

In 1947 about a quarter of sitting magistrates were over 70, and there were even some over 90. Only 12 per cent were under 50 and only just over one out of every 100 were under 40. That pattern has changed dramatically. Now 70 is the compulsory retiring age and no one is appointed for the first time above the age of 65. Today the average age of JPs is under 50 (exact statistics are not kept), thousands are under 40, and there are now even some magistrates in their late 20s. But the average age of benches is still not as low as the Lord Chancellor's department would like, in spite of efforts made to recruit younger JPs, in their 30s. For one thing, men and women with young families find it more difficult to devote their time to magisterial duties. Moreover, it is precisely at that period of their working lives that ambitious and able people are actively pursuing their careers. Although there is a certain prestige in becoming a magistrate, many employees feel that their regular absences would inevitably affect their chances of promotion. Self-employed, professional and business men and women simply cannot spare the time and loss of income which becoming a magistrate might entail. Women who did not work full-time used to be a traditional source for recruitment, but the pattern of the working husband and the non- or only part-time working wife is itself breaking down. Getting young magistrates is likely to continue to be a problem, but at least the public image of the magistrate of not so long ago – rubicund, elderly local squire, or crusty retired colonel – is now very far from the truth.

## Training

Only since 1966 have new justices of the peace received any compulsory training at all. What they get is relatively basic; it is not aimed at making them legal experts. The expertise in the law is provided by the legally qualified justices' clerk.

New magistrates are now being trained under a method (introduced in 1998) based on acquiring 'competences' in the various judicial skills and knowledge they need, as well as in their behaviour and attitude. The competences – which are accumulated on a sort of points system – are built up through attending talks (on such issues as ethnic awareness and poverty), background reading, and participating in discussions and practical exercises designed to develop their decision-making skills in dealing with bail applications, reaching a verdict and deciding on sentence. They will also visit courts, prisons, young offender institutions, the probation service and community service schemes.

New JPs are helped to develop their competences by senior magistrates, acting as mentors. They will be regularly appraised (at least every three years) by specially selected experienced magistrates, and could be asked to undergo further training if they're found wanting in any area.

It is too soon to assess whether this new training format will produce better magistrates. In any case the vast majority of magistrates we have today will have been trained under the old, far less structured system, but they'll be subject to regular appraisal and further training under the new system. Whichever form of training we look at, it still does not add up to anything like a professional education; but that's not the aim anyway, since the basis of the lay magistracy is judgment by people in the community on their peers.

How can we give such minimally trained people such awesome responsibilities? The answer is three-fold. First, the people chosen are supposed to have exhibited already in their careers, or in work for their community, or in some other way, the kind of qualities that will make them capable of judging and sentencing others with commonsense, fairness and understanding. Second, they can acquire the necessary skills, knowledge and experience gradually, from sitting on the bench as the junior member, under the guidance of more senior JPs. Third, they lean heavily on their legally qualified justices' clerk to give them the legal information they need.

## The justices' clerk

Our system of lay magistrates relies on professional back-up and administration. Someone has to run the shop, and it cannot be the amateurs. The 200 or so justices' clerks – who have to be barristers or solicitors – are the pivotal figures of the magistrates' courts. They're backed up by more than 2000 court legal advisers who are either lawyers or have a relevant diploma; the eventual aim is for all of them to be fully qualified lawyers.

The justice's clerk for each area is responsible for making his courts run efficiently; he's also the legal adviser and unofficial mentor to the magistrates, and their instructor, playing an important part in training them in their duties. But during the trial itself, his functions are circumscribed. Brian Harris QC, a former President of the Justices' Clerks Society, explains:

When he gives his advice it's very important that he shouldn't in any way express a view as to the facts of the case, because that's not for him. He mustn't give his assessment, even if he may have made one, on the credibility of the witnesses. He mustn't, even by the raising of an eyebrow, express disbelief in certain testimony. All that is for the magistrates to decide. But he must ensure that they understand the principles upon which they decide, the admissibility of the evidence upon which they are called to act. In other words, that they are in full possession of the proper legal principles upon which to act.

The justices' clerk has also been given some quasi-judicial functions himself – issuing warrants of arrest and granting legal aid, for instance. Lord Justice Auld's inquiry into the criminal courts procedure (see page 146) will be looking closely at the role played by the justices' clerk. One possible reform would be to allow him to be part of the magistrates' deliberations – after all, the justices' clerks have had greater experience of criminal trials and know more about the law and the court's powers than the magistrates themselves do.

## The stipendiary magistrate

The lay magistracy numbered over 30,000 in 1999. The stipendiaries – now officially called district judges (magistrates' courts) – who are paid, full-time, legally qualified magistrates, number around 100, half of them in London, the others dotted around some of the bigger urban centres. Originally appointed when the reputation of the lay magistracy was at a low ebb, the few stipendiaries have remained part of the system. For the most part, stipendiary and lay justices coexist reasonably happily together, even when they inhabit the same court.

It is accepted that stipendiaries dispense a different kind of justice from that meted out by part-time justices, though there is no agreement as to which is preferable. Some say that the full-time 'stipes' quickly become case-hardened, strict and tending not to believe defendants; others argue that they are much more efficient, professional and fair.

The top stipendiary magistrate is the Chief Metropolitan Magistrate, who sits at Bow Street Magistrates' Court. All extradition requests, such as those against the former Chilean dictator General Pinochet, have to be considered by him or another Bow Street magistrate.

## The future of the lay magistracy

The lay magistrates' system in England and Wales is undoubtedly very quick, very cheap, but pretty rough and ready.

Several criticisms are made against it. From the point of view of the users of magistrates' courts, whether as defendants, witnesses or other interested parties, magistrates' courts are said to be confusing, uninformative and lacking basic facilities. Attempts are being made to make courts more user-friendly by providing more information and more comforts and generally trying to make the courts less forbidding and unpleasant.

More important criticisms revolve around the quality of justice dished out by lay magistrates. It is said that they tend to be prosecution-minded and too inclined to believe police witnesses rather than the accused. That certainly used to be true, but nowadays magistrates are far more sceptical about police evidence than they were in the past. They no longer assume, as many did in former times, that the police always tell the truth and the accused invariably lies.

The third main criticism is that there is too much of a social barrier between the magistrates and the defendants in the dock. Black defendants, in particular, tend to mistrust magistrates' justice, and there are some research findings suggesting that blacks do seem to get a worse deal than whites – less likely to get bail than white defendants in similar circumstances, more likely to get a prison sentence for a similar crime. Magistrates are not wholly to blame. Part of the problem is that, not infrequently, the police charge blacks when they might not charge whites in similar circumstances; or charge them with more serious offences.

The fourth criticism is that magistrates are conviction-minded. The statistics show that an accused has a far better chance of being acquitted by a jury than by magistrates. The acquittal rate by juries in the Crown Courts is around 64 per cent; in the magistrates' courts – though no specific statistics are kept – it's generally accepted that fewer than one in five who plead not guilty are acquitted. Magistrates argue that this merely shows that they are less often taken in than juries, not that they are convicting innocent defendants. Fewer than three per cent of those convicted appeal, and fewer than 40 per cent of them succeed. But some critics believe that wrongful, as well as justified, convictions are more likely in magistrates' trials, mainly because magistrates' courts do not have the time to be as thorough.

Whatever its faults, most lawyers and others who have come into contact with the system believe that, on the whole, it works.

Magistrates deliver justice cheaply (proportionately, England has easily the lowest bill for judicial services of any developed country), and relatively speedily and efficiently. The lay magistracy does the job asked of it and it offers good value for money. No serious contenders have been proposed to replace it and it is likely to remain the corner-stone of our justice system for the foreseeable future. For one thing, it would be virtually impossible to find enough full-time legally qualified judges to replace the magistrates.

That doesn't mean that the magistracy can't be made more efficient. There is a running programme of reorganizing the courts, by abol-ishing some of them, amalgamating others, and generally reducing the number of courts and administrative regions – some of them unchanged since medieval times, but now being reduced to 42 so as to have the same boundaries as police and Crown Prosecution Service areas. Also under scrutiny is the balance between lay magistrates and stipendiaries.

Some of the initiatives have not gone down well with supporters of the traditional JPs system. They claim that the result may be a reduction in the quality of justice meted out and a threat to the magistrates' centuries-old independence from government, as well as the disintegration of the principle that magistrates dispense local, community-focused justice.

In particular, the financing of individual magistrates' courts is being linked to productivity and performance. Speed and quantity, critics fear, will become more important than justice.

Even though there is no question of a wholesale replacement of the lay magistracy with professional judges, some shift towards a more professional judiciary is probable. A Lord Chancellor's department committee is looking at the lay and the stipendiary magistracy to see whether the professionals should take on more of the work – at which they are more efficient than their lay equivalents. The Auld inquiry into the criminal courts (see page 146) will also be making recommendations on the same issue when it reports in 2001.

# CHAPTER VI

# The Criminal Process

John Smith is 36, married with two children. He is a contract furniture salesman, a job that involves him in 40,000 miles of driving a year. One November morning he leaves his house later than his usual eight o'clock. He is in a hurry. A few minutes later he is driving down Laurel Avenue and about to overtake a blue builders' van. Suddenly the van swerves out into the middle of the road and then turns sharply left into Cornwallis Road, which forms a T-junction with Laurel Avenue. Smith is forced out into the middle of the road. He cannot see whether anything is coming out of Cornwallis Road. As he passes the blue van, a motor-cycle suddenly appears in front of him. He takes what emergency action he can, and swerves out even further to the wrong side of the road. Somehow he misses the motor bike.

Anne Jones, aged 30, has just taken her five-year-old daughter, Katy, to school and is on her way to work. She is about to cross Laurel Avenue; she looks to both sides and steps off the kerb. Suddenly she becomes aware of a car bearing down on her at speed on the wrong side of the road. A split second later it hits her. She is lifted on to the bonnet and then thrown down into the gutter. She lies there, unconscious.

John Smith stops his car and rushes up to try to help. Eventually an ambulance is called to give Anne Jones medical attention. A policeman appears on the scene, and starts asking Smith and a nearby eye-witness about the accident.

From that moment on, John Smith, like around two million other people every year, finds himself embroiled in the criminal process. For the majority the involvement is slight. They may not even have to go to court. Most of those accused of minor traffic offences, for instance, can usually plead guilty by letter or, if they have to attend court, the case will be over quickly, and the sentence will be a small fine. What often matters is not the sentence itself, but the fact that it results in a criminal record that can have grave consequences for a person's career and reputation. The tiniest theft is still an offence of dishonesty, liable to bar the way to certain jobs. And even relatively trivial motoring offences can be significant if the driver needs his car for his livelihood. Perhaps even more important to some people is their standing among their friends, neighbours and colleagues. A moment's lapse resulting in a minor criminal charge can destroy a person's reputation and status where it counts most, in his community. So it is not just those accused of serious crime and facing possible imprisonment for whom the process of criminal justice is desperately frightening. It is a chastening experience for all but the most hardened offenders.

## The first steps

For John Smith the first formal step on the long and complex road to trial starts when the policeman called to the scene of the accident makes up his mind that Smith has probably committed an offence – either dangerous or careless driving. The moment he comes to this conclusion he has to administer this caution:

You do not have to say anything. But it may harm your defence if you do not when questioned mention something which you later rely on in court. Anything you do say may be given in evidence.

This does not mean that Smith will necessarily be prosecuted; sometimes the police will decide that there is not enough evidence. But the caution puts Smith on warning that he will probably face a charge. He decides to remain silent.

There are more dramatic ways of coming into conflict with the law, by being arrested for instance. Arrest is the process of placing someone suspected of a crime in legal custody. It can be done with the help of a warrant of arrest – a document signed by a magistrate when he has been persuaded by the police that there is enough evidence against the person involved. Nowadays warrants are not often used to arrest suspected criminals, though they continue to be issued when defendants out on bail fail to turn up.

Mostly, arrests are carried out without a warrant, by a policeman who reasonably suspects that a person has committed, is committing, or is about to commit a serious offence, one punishable by at least five years' imprisonment – the technical term is 'arrestable offence'. Then there are various specific laws allowing a policeman to arrest without warrant for some lesser offences. He must caution anyone he arrests. In addition, any individual has the right to arrest someone committing an arrestable offence. This is what is known as making a citizen's arrest.

## The decision to prosecute

The year 1986 saw one of the most fundamental reforms in the history of the English criminal justice system. Until then, the decision to prosecute was largely in the hands of the police. But that system was haphazard and inconsistent. The 43 police areas in England and Wales each had its own way of deciding on prosecution. Policies and arrangements differed.

An even more basic objection was identified by the Royal Commission on Criminal Procedure in 1981. It was not in the public interest or in the interests of justice, the Commission felt, that the very people who investigated a crime, and who were therefore committed to a particular view of it – the police – should also be the prosecuting authority. What was needed was an independent body to look at the evidence with a new eye and decide what charges were justified.

The result was the formation of a new Crown Prosecution Service (CPS) with the task of studying evidence gathered by the police and taking the decisions on whether or not to prosecute, and on what charges. The CPS, staffed by more than 2000 lawyers (both solicitors and barristers), is now, following changes in 1999, spread around 42 prosecution areas, each with its own Chief Crown Prosecutor. The national head of the service is the Director of Public Prosecutions (DPP), currently David Calvert-Smith QC, who, in turn, is responsible to the Attorney General.

The CPS has a great deal of discretion over whether or not to prosecute. There is no obligation to prosecute whenever a crime has been committed. Indeed, prosecuting all offenders would require many times the facilities and manpower available. There may be many reasons for not prosecuting: the defendant is very old or seriously ill; he is only a trivial cog in a larger wheel and the ringleaders are not being prosecuted; the offence was committed a very long time ago. More importantly, crown prosecutors or the DPP might think that, although they are pretty sure who the criminal is, there is not quite enough evidence to get a conviction. There must be 'a realistic prospect of conviction', which means that there must be a better chance of conviction than acquittal – more than a 50 per cent chance.

The CPS does not deal with all decisions to prosecute. For certain categories of serious crime, it is necessary to get the consent of the Attorney General, and that has not changed under the new system. Examples include offences of terrorism and offences under the Official Secrets Act. The Attorney General is also consulted on cases of national sensitivity or notoriety; and he retains the power to stop prosecutions already begun.

The Attorney General and his deputy, the Solicitor General, are politicians, appointed from among the senior barrister MPs or peers of the party in power. Apart from his role in the courts, the Attorney General has a political role, advising the government on legal matters and answering questions in Parliament. Lord Williams of Mostyn is currently Attorney General and Ross Cranston Solicitor General.

There are all sorts of other authorities which can launch prosecutions – among them the Inland Revenue, Customs and Excise, the Department of Social Security (for social security frauds) and local authorities. Private individuals as well can bring prosecutions, though there are safeguards to prevent private citizens from abusing the legal process to feed their personal obsessions. Private prosecutions by individuals are mainly for assault, when the CPS have decided not to prosecute, but there have also been the more spectacular cases, such as that brought in 1979 by the morality campaigner Mary Whitehouse, against *Gay News* for blasphemy. Other examples of private prosecutions include one brought by a mother against a man who supplied her son with the drugs that led to his death, and several brought by the parents of children killed in road accidents against the allegedly drunk or dangerous driver responsible. The parents of Stephen Lawrence, the black youth murdered in a racial attack in South London in 1993, brought an unsuccessful private prosecution against some of the men suspected of the killing.

Once the decision to prosecute has been taken, the suspect can be told of it in two ways: by a charge or a summons. For serious crimes there will usually be a charge following arrest. The police will tell the suspect that he is being charged with the particular offence. Once again they must caution him, and tell him that he needn't say anything. The summons is a formal document used in less serious cases, ordering the defendant to appear in court on a specified day to answer the charge against him. The summons can be served on the defendant personally, but sometimes it can even be sent by post, for minor motoring offences for instance.

## Bail

For serious crimes, the police usually arrest the suspect and keep him in detention until charging him. After being charged an accused, if not given bail by the police, must appear before a magistrates' court 'as soon as practicable', which in practice usually means the day after the charge (or two days if that day is a Sunday). The magistrates then have to decide whether to allow the accused out on bail or remand him in custody in one of the remand prisons for those awaiting trial. The law, the Bail Act 1976, says that magistrates should grant bail except in certain circumstances, the main examples being if they think that the accused is unlikely to turn up for his trial, or will interfere with witnesses, or will commit offences if let out, or needs to be in custody for his own protection.

Obviously the more serious the offence the more likely he is to disappear or nobble witnesses. By law, defendants charged with murder, attempted murder, manslaughter, rape or attempted rape, will almost always be refused bail. Alleged armed robbers are also unlikely to get it. Nor will there be a right to bail for anyone accused of committing an offence while already on bail for another offence.

Apart from the seriousness of the offence, the magistrates have to make the best assessment they can about the accused – his record, his job, his personal circumstances and so on. A police objection to bail will usually weigh strongly with the magistrates, but they must not refuse bail merely because the police say so; there must be a valid reason for it.

Magistrates have been criticized from both sides for their bail decisions. The police claim that they let out too many on bail, and every now and again there are claims by senior police officers and stories in the newspapers about people who commit a string of offences, or sometimes even murder, while out on bail. They paint a picture of gullible magistrates conned into releasing burglars and violent criminals to commit more crimes.

On the other side it is claimed that too few people are getting bail, and the picture drawn there is of thousands of people languishing for weeks and months behind bars and then at their trial being acquitted, or, if convicted, given a non-custodial sentence.

An accused remanded in custody awaiting his trial used to have to appear in court at least every eight days, but there are now many exceptions to that rule, and it is now most common for remands to be made for 28 days at a time.

If magistrates grant bail they can impose conditions; for instance, that the accused must not frequent a particular pub, or must hand in his passport, or must report regularly to the police. They can ask for sureties – people who stake their own money on the expectation that the accused will turn up for his trial. If he doesn't, they can lose their money. Many trusting friends and relatives have lost their life savings this way.

## Committal

Whether a crime is tried in the magistrates' court or the Crown Court depends on its classification. Certain types of offence are 'triable either way', either summary trial by the justices, or trial by jury. Dangerous driving is one such offence. Theft is another. At the time of writing, the law gives the defendant the right to insist on a jury trial, but a bill going through parliament at the time of writing would controversially remove that unfettered right, and give the decision to the magistrates. For other specified offences, there is no choice. They are either 'summary', the less serious, tried by magistrates, or 'indictable', serious offences tried in the Crown Court. The vast majority of cases stay in the magistrates' court. But where a case is triable by the Crown Court, it is usually committed there by the magistrates' court, which has the duty to assess whether there is enough evidence to warrant sending the accused for trial by jury. In theory, only when the magistrates are satisfied that there is enough evidence – a *prima facie* case – will they commit to the Crown Court, though in practice committal proceedings have become largely automatic.

Traditionally, they were supposed to be a filter through which every serious charge passed to ensure that only genuine cases got to the higher court, and that prosecutions not backed by enough evidence were stopped. The intention was that committal proceedings would be a safeguard for the defendant, to allow worthless or malicious prosecutions against him to be nipped in the bud. In the past, it was not unusual for prosecution witnesses to give evidence in the witness box and be subject to cross-examination. This happened, for instance, when the former leader of the Liberal Party, Jeremy Thorpe, faced charges of conspiracy to murder in 1979. He was eventually committed for trial at the Old Bailey, where he was acquitted. Nowadays, committal proceedings with witnesses in person have all but disappeared.

In the vast majority of cases magistrates (with the agreement of the defendant and his lawyer) can commit to the Crown Court without even considering the evidence.

A further inroad into committal proceedings has been introduced in respect of complicated fraud trials. These no longer have any committal stage at all. Provided a senior official like the DPP or the Director of the Serious Fraud Office approves, such fraud trials can be sent to the Crown Court from the start, without magistrates having a look at the evidence first and without the defence having the chance to test it. That is what has happened in the Maxwell, Guinness, Blue Arrow, and other recent complex fraud cases.

The practice of sending cases directly to the Crown Court, by-passing committal proceedings before the magistrates, has spread to other serious offences (armed robbery and rape among them), and it is likely that this will become the norm in 2001.

John Smith's case is rather less spectacular. He turns up in court with his solicitor for his straightforward automatic committal. The charge – dangerous driving – is read to him. The magistrates' clerk explains that he has the choice of having the case heard before the magistrates or going to the Crown Court and having a jury trial. He goes on to tell Smith that even if he chooses summary trial before the magistrates, he may be sent to the Crown Court for sentence if the magistrates think the circumstances warrant a longer sentence than they have the power to pass. Smith answers that he wishes to be tried by a jury. After a few formalities, the magistrates then formally commit Smith to the Crown Court. The proceedings have taken exactly five minutes.

If the Criminal Justice (Mode of Trial) Bill becomes law, it will not be so easy for defendants such as Smith. It would be for the magistrates to decide whether to try the case at the magistrates' court or commit him to the Crown Court. In coming to their decision, they would have to take into account all the circumstances to do with the offence – how serious is it? The defendant would have the chance to put his case for being allowed trial by jury; if the magistrates refused, there would be a right of appeal to a Crown Court judge.

# The trial

Eight centuries ago the main method of deciding guilt or innocence in England was trial by ordeal. An accused was given a red hot poker to hold, or his hands were scalded with boiling water. His injuries were immediately bandaged and the bandages were removed three days later. If the wound had healed, he was innocent; if not, he was guilty. In 1215, Pope Innocent III condemned trial by ordeal and it soon ceased to be the main mode of trial.

Trial by battle, which was current at the same time, was an even cruder device. An accused could call on his accuser (an individual in those days, not the state) to engage in a fight to the death. Astonishingly, trial by battle was not formally abolished until 1819, following a case where a bricklayer, Abraham Thornton, was accused of murder by William Ashford, the victim's brother. Thornton demanded the right to trial by battle and the courts found to their surprise that the statute granting it had not been repealed. The battle never took place, however, and Thornton eventually fled to America.

There were other primitive modes of determining innocence or guilt: getting 12 oath-swearers to confirm innocence was one. Such was the religious fear of swearing a false oath that a man's guilt could be assumed from his failure to get enough people to attest to his innocence. Another way was to make an accused swear that he was innocent, and then immediately eat some dry bread – if his oath was false, he would choke.

Trial by jury started taking over from these ancient forms from the reign of Henry II in the twelfth century. But the jury was a very different body then. It was made up of people who knew the accused – his friends and neighbours – not, as today, people who specifically must not know the defendant. Those who refused trial by jury for felonies (serious crimes) were forced to lie down and heavy weights were pressed on them until they consented to trial, or died. Some preferred to die, because then at least they died unconvicted and their goods passed on to their families instead of being confiscated.

While, over the centuries, the criminal trial has become more sophisticated and its procedures more balanced to achieve justice, the inherent concept of a combat, a contest, has remained the feature throughout. There is a challenger – the accuser – and a defender. Instead of swords and lances the weapons are facts and legal arguments. Each side has its champion, the lawyer. There is an arbiter to make sure that the contest is fought fairly according to law – the judge.

To the casual observer the trial still appears like a strange ritual in which the judge, the lawyers and, to some extent, the court officials are participants but the rest, including the accused and the jury, are excluded.

There are remnants of medieval language used. Judges and barristers continue to wear costumes appropriate to a different century. Above all, it becomes clear that there are two languages being spoken. The judge and barristers use one, and everyone else another. The language of the law is ultra-polite. A reprimand or criticism is delivered in such superficially amiable terms that only those who speak the language realize the sting. Senior judges are addressed as 'My Lord' (or M'Lud, as it is traditionally supposed to sound, but rarely does) even though they are not peers. Junior judges are 'your honour'. Barristers refer to each other as 'my learned friend', even in the heat of a dispute; a judge's opinion or remark, however ludicrous or outrageous, is always treated 'with respect' or even 'with the greatest respect', however far that may be from the truth. Lawyers speak, even when they are addressing witnesses, in an old-fashioned convoluted way seldom used in real life. The fact is that the barristers and the judge belong to the same club; they follow its rules and keep its traditions, and non-members cannot be party to the ritual. Defendants in criminal trials and litigants in civil cases are often disconcerted and upset by the apparent chumminess between lawyers who they think ought to be passionately antagonistic.

The criminal process in our 'adversarial' system concentrates heavily on what happens during the trial itself. Of course investigations have been made beforehand, mainly by the police, and also by those representing the defence. But, in contrast to the continental inquisitorial system, very little is cut and dried by the time of the trial. The verdict will depend on a combination of factors: the strength of the evidence obviously, but also the skill and persuasive abilities of the respective advocates; how the witnesses perform in the witness box (it is an unfortunate and unfair fact that a persuasive witness may not necessarily be telling the truth, and a nervous-looking, shifty, hesitant witness may be utterly honest); what impression the accused makes; how the judge controls the trial, how much he intervenes and what he includes in his summing-up; and the composition, intelligence and attitudes of the jury.

## The day of the trial

It is 10.30 in the morning, the time when Crown Courts all around the country start their main business of the day. The clerk of the court, an usher or two and the court stenographer or, more often nowadays, the person in charge of the recording equipment, are in their places. The barristers for the prosecution and the defence, wigged and gowned, are sitting in a row set aside for counsel. Behind the barristers sit the solicitors or, more likely, their clerks – Mr Short, John Smith's solicitor, is too busy to come to court for such a relatively uncomplicated case. The jury box is empty. So is the dock, except for a court officer.

The judge is announced with the admonition of 'court rise' or 'be upstanding in court'. Everyone stands up. He enters from a separate door at the back of the court and sits down. The clerk of the court calls Smith's name and he comes into the dock. After confirming his identity the clerk reads the charge:

John Smith, you are charged that on the 14th day of November last you drove a motor vehicle on a road, namely Laurel Avenue, London W3, dangerously, contrary to Section 2 of the Road Traffic Act 1988.

He ends with the time-honoured formula: 'Are you guilty or not guilty?' John Smith answers firmly: 'Not guilty'. If he had pleaded guilty (as around 70 per cent of Crown Court defendants do) all that would be left of the trial would be the procedure leading to sentence. Smith's not guilty plea is followed by the swearing-in of the jury. When the 12 men and women have finally been sworn the trial recommences. The clerk tells the jury what the charge against Smith is. The preliminary stage – the overture – is ended. Act One of the drama commences.

## The prosecution case

Mr White, the barrister for the prosecution, stands up and makes what is called an opening speech. 'The right to begin is a priceless and too often squandered asset,' says Richard Du Cann QC in *The Art of the Advocate* (Penguin, 1993). Mr White explains the circumstances of the accident, with the help of a plan, copies of which are given to the jury. He goes on to summarize the evidence that he will call on behalf of the prosecution. He tells them what witnesses he will call and the gist of what they will say – or rather, what he expects them to say. But he doesn't know for sure. A witness may not say exactly what counsel expects, or may recant some of his evidence under cross-examination by the defence. The whole concept of an opening speech by the prosecution has been criticized as giving them an unfair advantage – the jury may take more notice of what the prosecution foretell about the evidence than what the witnesses actually say.

After that, prosecuting counsel tells the jury that it is for the prosecution to prove that the accused committed the crime. It is not for the accused to prove his innocence. This is fundamental to the English trial and the jury will be reminded of this principle many times during the trial. Prosecution counsel explains that they must be sure of the accused's guilt, 'beyond reasonable doubt'. After explaining that 'standard of proof', as it is called, he gives them the definition of dangerous driving and explains what has to be proved.

*MR WHITE*: Well, ladies and gentlemen, there are principally two things which you have to decide before you could come to the conclusion that Mr Smith had driven dangerously.

Now, what does 'dangerous' mean? Well, what the law says is that there has to be a danger either of injury to any person or of serious damage to property. It will be up to you to decide whether the defendant's driving did create such a danger of personal injury or serious physical damage. You will hear – and indeed it is not contested by the defence – that the defendant's driving did indeed cause injury to Mrs Anne Jones. But that is not the end of the matter. Even if you decide that the defendant's driving did create the danger of injury, that is not the end of the matter. You will then go on to consider a second question.

The law says that a person is to be regarded as driving dangerously if, in all the circumstances, he drives far below what would be expected of a competent and careful driver, and that it would be obvious to a competent and careful driver that driving in that way would be dangerous.

He goes on explaining the law and summarizing the evidence he expects to call. The prosecution's opening speech may take minutes, hours, or even, in complicated cases, days. Not surprisingly, perhaps, the 1993 Royal Commission on Criminal Justice's proposal that the limit should usually be 15 minutes did not go down at all well with prosecution counsel.

His opening speech over, prosecuting counsel starts calling his witnesses. They will usually include a police officer or two, the victim of the crime, and any witnesses who can shed light on it, eye-witnesses particularly. There may also be expert witnesses, on fingerprints for instance. In John Smith's case there are only three witnesses – the policeman at the scene; Anne Jones, the injured victim; and Mrs Wright, who was about to cross Laurel Avenue when John Smith passed in his car. She claims he was going at excessive speed and nearly knocked her over.

The witnesses first take the oath, according to the customs of their religion, or they solemnly affirm, if they are non-believers. The Christian oath, the one most widely taken, states: 'I swear by almighty God that the evidence I shall give shall be the truth, the whole truth and nothing but the truth.' (There is no 'So help me God'.) The taking of the oath marks the moment from which a lying witness can be prosecuted for perjury.

The questions put to a witness and the answers he gives are collectively known as examination-in-chief. This is where the prosecution elicits the basic facts. It is a cardinal rule that the barrister must not put words into his witness' mouth; he must not, as it is called, 'lead' his witness. It is in order for Mr White to ask Mrs Wright what happened next and get the reply: 'The accused's car nearly knocked me over.' But he is not entitled to ask: 'Did the accused's car nearly knock you over?' That would be a 'leading' question, and not allowed.

Prosecution counsel's task is to elicit all the relevant facts from the witnesses – he has a duty not to extract only the evidence damaging to the accused. The law steps in to stop the witness from saying something which he does not know for himself – 'hearsay' evidence. This is what the witness has heard from someone else, not something which he can vouch for himself. For instance, a witness' evidence that someone told him that Smith was driving fast because he was in a hurry would not be admissible.

In John Smith's case neither the policeman's evidence nor that of Anne Jones will be controversial. Mrs Jones remembers very little of the accident. Mrs Wright's evidence, however, is potentially damaging, because it suggests that Smith was driving far too fast even before the events leading to the accident.

*MRS WRIGHT*: Well, I decided that I'd cross the road, just a few yards down from my home, and go across to the other side of the road, and this van passed me. And I was just about to cross when this red car came zooming past, nearly knocked me down actually . . .

After she has given her basic evidence, it is the turn of Smith's barrister to cross-examine her. The object of cross-examination is simple: it is to destroy, discredit or at least cast doubt on the evidence of the other side's witness, and in weakening the opponent's case to enhance your own side's. The art of cross-examination is not easy. In the hands of a skilled practitioner it is a sleek rapier delicately thrusting, testing, tempting, looking for an opening and, when finding one, directing the blade home cleanly and irrevocably. But in the hands of an inexperienced or second-rate advocate it is more like a blunderbuss, peppering shot everywhere, almost at random, occasionally, through luck and statistical probability, hitting a target, but often causing much damage on the way. Cross-examination is bounded by a host of detailed rules about what the cross-examiner may and may not ask.

He is, however, free to ask leading questions, an important tool in his attempt to break down the witness. The cross-examination is rarely as quickly effective and as crude as it is portrayed in television drama. Witnesses seldom fall to pieces because of one question. Rather it is the accumulation of threads which, when skilfully woven together, portray to the jury a witness whose evidence, seeming so strong a little while ago, suddenly appears unreliable, possibly mistaken or even, perhaps, untruthful.

Defence counsel, Mr Brown, is anxious to demonstrate to the jury that Mrs Wright is not a witness they should believe. He asks her to estimate the speeds and distances; he puts to her contradictions between her statement to the police and her evidence in court.

When defence counsel has finished cross-examining the witness, prosecution counsel is entitled to re-examine, to try to clear up, and put in the best light, any new matter that has come out of cross-examination, and to recover any ground that might have been lost.

And so the prosecution case continues: examination-in-chief of prosecution witnesses, cross-examination by the defence and possible re-examination by the prosecution.

The judge can, and often does, intervene to ask questions of his own when he is not clear on a point, or to supplement a line of questioning started by the barristers. But a judge must not take over the case. Our adversarial system requires that the combatants should be the prosecution and the defence – the judge should not himself descend into the arena.

The first scene of Act One draws to a close. Prosecution counsel has finished calling his witnesses and formally announces: 'That is the case for the prosecution.'

## The defence case

It is now the defence's turn. But before calling his witnesses the defence counsel has a chance of ending the whole trial there and then by persuading the judge (in the absence of the jury) that the prosecution has not even produced enough evidence to warrant going further. There is no case to meet, he suggests; no reasonable jury could convict on the evidence that the prosecution has put forward. There is no *prima facie* case. Defence counsel will obviously minimize the effect of the evidence which has been given, while the prosecution barrister will emphasize its strength. If the judge decides in favour of the defence, he will call the jury in and tell them formally to acquit the accused. Otherwise, the case goes on. (Even then, the defence counsel may choose to call no witnesses in the confidence that the prosecution has not discharged the burden of proof, and therefore that the jury will be bound to find in favour of the accused.)

In John Smith's case there is no point in suggesting that there is no case to answer – the fact that he has knocked down a pedestrian while travelling on the wrong side of the road is at least a *prima facie* indication of dangerous or careless driving.

Mr Brown opens the defence case by calling John Smith as his first witness. He does not make an opening speech. Unless the accused is going to be the only witness, defence counsel are entitled to outline their case, just as the prosecution do for the other side. But they often forgo their right. Except in a complicated case, a defence opening address is usually considered unnecessary.

The accused is usually the first witness called. But there is no obligation on him to give evidence at all. He has the right to say nothing – the so-called right to silence, which has been part of English law for centuries. This right has now been greatly diminished by a 1994 law. It meant not just that an accused had the right to say nothing – no one can be forced to speak – but that his silence couldn't be held against him. So if he refused to answer questions the police put to him under interrogation, or, later, if he chose not to go into the witness box at his trial, neither the prosecution nor the judge was allowed to make any adverse comment to the jury about his failure to answer questions or give evidence. They couldn't suggest to the jury, for instance, that an innocent person would have been prepared to speak and that therefore a failure to do so might be an indication of guilt. That has now changed. The words of the police caution to suspects now include 'It may harm your defence if you do not when questioned mention something which you later rely on in court . . .';

and the prosecution and judges are, in some circumstances (the law on this is complicated), allowed to tell the jury that they are entitled to draw adverse inferences from an accused's failure to give an explanation.

The accused is followed by the witnesses in support of his case. The procedure of the first part of the trial is reversed: defence counsel examines his witnesses and then prosecution counsel has the chance to cross-examine them, to try to undo or reverse any harm to his case that defence counsel may have done. There may be re-examination by the defence, and some questions from the judge.

John Smith's own evidence is aimed at trying to persuade the jury that he was not driving dangerously. He claims that he was placed in an unforeseeable emergency and had to take evading action, because of the van that suddenly swerved and the motor-cycle that appeared from Cornwallis Road.

*JOHN SMITH*: I was thinking about overtaking, and at that point the van moved out suddenly to the right, and then swung away quickly to the left, without any signal. And this manoeuvre by the van prompted me to swing quickly to the right and avoid it.

As I overtook the van, as I drew level with it, a motor-cyclist suddenly appeared right in front of me. I'm assuming it came from my left, although I never saw it actually move. It was suddenly in front of me. I was slightly towards the crown of the road, and the motor-cycle was dead in front of me at this point, just a matter of yards, and I jammed my foot on the brakes and turned quickly to the right, and began to skid. I missed the motor-cycle . . .

Later, Mr Brown asks him: 'What caused you to brake and swerve in the manner we've heard about?'

*JOHN SMITH*: The combination of the sudden manoeuvre of the van, and the appearance of the motor-cyclist directly in front of me.

He is cross-examined by Mr White, who suggests that he was driving at excessive speed, that he should not have overtaken the van in the first place, and that, had he been driving at normal speed, he would have been able to stop behind the turning van and avoid the accident.

*MR WHITE*: You see what I'm putting to you, Mr Smith, is that in fact your speed was such that the van slowing down and turning to the left either meant you ran into the back of the van, because you were too close, going too fast; or you had to do what you did, which was to swing out on to the wrong side of the road, without really being able to see what was coming. Now isn't that really what happened?

He then concentrates his cross-examination on the motor-cycle:

Mr Smith, you've heard the two witnesses giving their evidence, Mrs Wright, particularly, saying she didn't see any motor-cycle. Are you sure there was a motor-cycle there?
*JOHN SMITH*: There would have been no other reason for me to brake. Or to swerve.
*MR WHITE* (a little later): You see I suggest to you, Mr Smith, that this motor-cycle is really a figment of your imagination, something you've conjured up to explain why you took the action you did. Isn't that right?

Smith denies this firmly.

Now, to the surprise of the prosecution, the next witness is Timothy Wood, the driver of the blue van, who has only just been traced, partly the result of hard work by Smith's solicitor, Mr Short, and an inquiry agent, and partly through luck. Wood confirms Smith's story about the motor-cycle – up to that time one of the crucial elements of the case. There is little Mr White can do in cross-examination. One of the mainstays of his case has been undermined. The van driver is the second and last witness for the defence. The defence case is formally closed.

## Closing speeches

The witnesses have gone, the witness box is empty. The jury have been told all the evidence they need (or rather, all they are going to hear, which under the adversarial system may well amount to less than all the relevant evidence). It is now time for the barristers to take centre stage with no one to interrupt them. Prosecuting counsel is first. The defence then has the last word. It is the defence case that will be the more recent in the jury's mind, unless it is undone by the judge's summing-up which follows.

Both barristers will have the same objective: to summarize their side's case in its most favourable light; to highlight its strengths, play down its weaknesses; to boost the evidence given by their own witnesses and pick holes in the opposition's evidence. In the not too distant past, up to 40 years ago, a closing speech was the occasion for advocates to rise to the heights of their oratorical powers. This was part of the trial when the spotlight was on them and them alone, the chance to use all their verbal skills, their thespian talents, their powers to evoke sympathy and emotion, all to the service of their client. Usually it was the defence lawyer who had the best lines, but he also had the greatest responsibility. A poor performance on his part might have meant the gallows for his client. In that atmosphere thrived some of England's greatest advocates – Carson, Marshall Hall, Birkett, Hastings. It was Marshall Hall who finished his speech in defence of a pathetic ageing prostitute accused of murder with the exhortation:

Look at her, gentlemen of the jury. Look at her. God never gave her a chance. Won't you?

Can there have been a dry eye in the jury box? Whatever the effect such perorations had on the juries of yesteryear, they would probably only bring ridicule today. The barristers of today are perhaps more careful with their facts, more clinical in their analysis, more meticulous in their preparation, but utterly grey in their presentation to the jury. The late Richard Du Cann QC, one of England's most elegant advocates, bemoaned the increasing number of counsel who 'stumble through the odious task of addressing the judge, boring themselves almost as much as their audience'.

The points to be made in John Smith's case are obvious.

*FOR THE PROSECUTION*: But, ladies and gentlemen, isn't this really the situation – given the speed that you know he was travelling at, is it not simply that he had failed to give himself sufficient distance behind the van, and that when the emergency arose, and it wasn't you may think a particularly uncommon or extraordinary circumstance, he was simply going too fast to do the obvious and safe thing, which was to slow down in his own lane by braking, until the road was clear. Ladies and gentlemen, you may think if he'd done that, he would never have needed to leave his side of the road, and no accident would in fact have taken place . . .

His evidence, and it's quite unequivocal in my submission, is that he was forced to take evasive action by the action of the van and the motor-cycle. Prosecution would suggest to you that really the only reason he had to take evasive action was because he was going too fast to do the sensible and reasonable thing, of slowing down.

*FOR THE DEFENCE*: This defendant is faced with a very real emergency. He puts on his brakes; he avoids the motor-cyclist, the motor-cyclist carries on, and this defendant – doing the best he can, we submit – brakes but unfortunately strikes the unfortunate lady who you saw give evidence.

Members of the jury, can you really say that in the circumstances this defendant was driving in such a way as to create an obvious danger of causing personal injury, which is what the definition of dangerous driving requires? He was faced, in our submission, with these two unforeseen circumstances. First of all, he didn't know the van was going to turn, there was no indication.

Second unforeseen circumstance: the motor-cycle, waiting at the junction of Cornwallis Road, pulls out quite suddenly and quite wrongly into the main road, immediately in front of the defendant.

Members of the jury, bearing in mind all the circumstances of this case, we submit to you that the case is very far from being made out against this defendant . . .

In all the circumstances, I submit to you that there's only one proper verdict in this case, and this is one of 'Not Guilty'. Thank you.

Prosecution and defence counsel have finished their speeches, but the jury is not yet free. It is now time for the judge to address them.

## The judge's summing-up

The jury has heard an opening and a closing speech for the prosecution, a closing speech by the defence and a procession of witnesses giving evidence and being cross-examined. It might be thought that the issues in the case were firmly fixed in their minds. But they are to hear more. The judge is to sum up the case to them. What function does the summing-up serve?

First, its importance lies in the fact that it comes from an impartial independent source. The prosecution and the defence are the combatants, each fighting for their cause. They are not and cannot be expected to be impartial in their presentation of the case. The judge, on the other hand, is an independent figure, who can be trusted to summarize the main issues of the case impartially.

Second, the jury is made up of lay people, not lawyers. But some of the decisions they may have to make involve some appreciation of the legal niceties: what is the dividing line between dangerous driving and careless driving? How vital is it that the person *intends* to commit the crime with which he is charged? Again, a judge is a better guide through this legal minefield than counsel. Third, it is especially helpful in a long trial to have someone of experience highlighting the main points of the evidence which the jury may have forgotten because they were raised several days before and have not been mentioned by either counsel in closing speeches.

The judge will usually start by reminding the jury of the two essential aspects of the English criminal trial. First, that it is for the jury and only the jury to decide questions of fact and to make up their minds between the versions that have been put forward by the competing interests. The judge's role is limited to deciding legal issues and he should not trespass into the jury's province and express obvious views on the facts or the witnesses, and certainly not on the result. He sometimes does so, but the jury is entitled to, and should, disregard his opinion.

Second, the judge repeats that it is for the prosecution to prove guilt, so that the jury are sure of it, and not for the defence to prove innocence:

*JUDGE*: You could come to the conclusion – and I'm not going to say to you that you should, because that's a matter entirely for you – you might come to the conclusion that he was innocent of any offence at all, in which case the verdict would be 'Not Guilty'.

Secondly, you might come to the conclusion that although there was a strong suspicion of guilt, that nevertheless there was a reasonable doubt, and if there's a reasonable doubt in a case, well then the defendant is entitled to be acquitted.

The third possibility is that you might be satisfied so that you're sure that an offence had been committed, and if it has been committed, then it's your duty in accordance with your oaths to find a verdict of 'Guilty'.

The judge then defines the law of the offence charged. Sometimes it's simple. The definition of, say, burglary is relatively easy to explain. But where there are several charges, some of them alternatives to each other – murder and manslaughter for instance – it becomes very important for the judge to make his explanations clear. If he gets it wrong and misleads the jury on the law, it could be the basis for a successful appeal.

In John Smith's case there is an important legal point to be made. Although Smith has been charged with dangerous driving, the jury is entitled to acquit him on that, and yet find him guilty of the lesser charge of careless driving. What is the difference? The judge explains:

*JUDGE*: To find the defendant guilty of dangerous driving you must first be sure that he was driving in such a manner as to create a risk of causing physical injury to someone or serious damage to property, far below the standard expected of a competent and careful driver. Secondly, you must be sure that it would have been obvious to a careful and competent driver that the way he was driving was dangerous. The test is not whether this particular man thought he was driving dangerously. It is not this defendant's opinion of his driving that counts. The test is an objective one. Ladies and gentlemen, you have to ask yourself, would a careful and competent driver have realized that he was driving in a dangerous manner? If your answer is yes to both those questions, then you must find the defendant guilty of dangerous driving. If you are not sure that he is guilty of that offence, then you must find him not guilty.

But even if you decide that he is not guilty of dangerous driving, you may still think that he is guilty of the less serious offence of careless driving. Now careless driving, members of the jury, is defined as driving without due care and attention, or without reasonable consideration for other persons using the road. You will see from that that the test for careless driving, unlike that

117

for dangerous driving, does not require any evidence that the driver was endangering either people or property. What you have to ask yourself is: did this driver fall short of the normal standards of a reasonable prudent driver and drive in a way which you would regard as careless, not paying proper attention to his driving, or was the way he was driving inconsiderate to other persons – drivers in other cars, or pedestrians or cyclists or anyone else using the road? It does not matter whether or not he intended to drive carelessly. The question is: did he? And if you are satisfied that the defendant drove carelessly, without due care and attention, or without the consideration to other road users that drivers should show, then you must find him guilty of careless driving.

After explaining the law, the judge summarizes what he sees as the main points of the evidence. Throughout the trial he has taken notes (often in laborious longhand, one of the reasons why trials take so long; more and more judges, though, take notes on their laptop computers). He goes through his notes reminding the jury of the main factual issues. If there is more than one defendant, he must be particularly careful that he correctly distinguishes what evidence applies to which defendant.

At the end of his summing-up – which may take anything from a few minutes to a few days – he tells the jury that they must try to reach a unanimous verdict. It will only be hours later, if the jury have not been able to agree on their decision, that the judge may call them back to tell them that they can reach a majority verdict by a margin of ten to two or eleven to one.

The judge leaves the court. The jury file out. The accused is led away from the dock. The lawyers chat a little among themselves and slowly make their way out, as do the accused's friends and relatives and other spectators. The court is virtually empty. Outside it, the main participants and interested parties mill around. There is time for a cup of tea, but they cannot stay away too long in case of a speedy verdict. The curtain comes down on the first act.

## The verdict

The second act takes place almost entirely behind closed doors. The 12 members of the jury are taken to the room in which, in secret, they will reach their verdict. There they will stay for minutes, hours, or even days. If they couldn't reach their verdict within a day, they used to be put up overnight at a nearby posh hotel; nowadays they are allowed to go home for the night, after being warned not to discuss the case with anyone. In John Smith's trial, the jury need only an hour for their deliberations. They reach a unanimous verdict and tell the jury bailiff that they are ready to come back to court. The word spreads. The judge and the barristers are found. John Smith is brought back into the dock. The judge sits down and the jury file in.

*CLERK OF THE COURT*: Will the foreman please stand. Will you please confine yourself to answering my first question, yes or no. Has the jury reached a verdict upon which you are all agreed?
*FOREMAN*: We have.
*CLERK*: Do you find the defendant John Smith guilty or not guilty of dangerous driving?
*FOREMAN*: Not guilty.
*CLERK*: Do you find the defendant guilty or not guilty of careless driving?
*FOREMAN*: Guilty.
*CLERK*: Is that the verdict of you all?
*FOREMAN*: It is.
*CLERK*: Thank you, do sit down.

## Juries

An essential bulwark against oppression or an inefficient anachronism? Lord Devlin put it at its highest in *Trial By Jury* (Methuen, 1966):

The first object of any tyrant in Whitehall would be to make Parliament utterly subservient to his will; and the next to overthrow or diminish trial by jury, for no tyrant could afford to leave a subject's freedom in the hands of twelve of his countrymen. So that trial by jury is more than an instrument of justice and more than one wheel of the constitution: it is the lamp that shows that freedom lives.

One appeal court judge gave a more prosaic reason for praising the jury:

It has the great merit and advantage of being anonymous and amorphous. Once the trial is over it's dissolved and there is no person responsible to anybody or answerable for the decision. It can therefore be much more independent. It hasn't got to consider what people will think about it as an individual, as a judge might think about how the public will regard him as an individual, if he were to come to a wrong verdict.

The case against the jury was pithily put by the late Professor Brian Hogan, author of one of the leading academic works on criminal law:

Trial by jury has long outlived its usefulness. We preserve it because it's a sacred cow. It's been with us for so long and we're failing to look carefully into it, to see what it does, and to see whether there are rational grounds for defending it.

  If we'd never had trial by jury in this country and our practice had been to try cases by judges, rationally finding the facts and drawing inferences, and I were to come boldly along with the suggestion that this professional judgment should be replaced by an almost inscrutable verdict, by the first twelve men and women you meet in the street, I think any sensible person would believe that I'd gone out of my mind.

The police too, who admittedly have a particular interest to defend, have largely turned against the system. Juries acquit too many guilty criminals, they believe.

  It is not just a question of lawyers and judges versus academics and the police. Supporters and detractors of the system are to be found in all camps, including jurors themselves. Nor is it a stark question of the jury's survival or its abolition. Some of the criticisms could easily be met by reforms of particular aspects of the system, without the need to kill the institution altogether.

  Juries have been around for 800 years, but their functions and composition have changed considerably over that period. One of the most significant changes to the jury system took place in 1973. The theory is that juries are supposed to be chosen at random as representatives of the community, but this has never been so in practice. Before 1973 there was an age qualification and a property qualification. A juror had to be between 21 and 60 and a house owner or ratepayer. This test discriminated against women, mainly because many married couples had their houses in the husband's name, and against the young, who were not householders. A pre-1973 jury was therefore predominantly male and middle-aged – hardly representative of the community.

This has changed dramatically. Now jury service is based on the electoral roll, which means that an 18-year-old can serve on a jury. The maximum age is 70. Selection is done according to a formula (based on the electoral register) impossible to rig, and confirmed by the Royal Statistical Society as delivering a random result. If some people have been called up three times and others never, it's a statistical coincidence, not human tampering.

There are categories of people who cannot serve on a jury: judges, magistrates, lawyers, the police, prison warders and others connected with the administration of justice; the clergy; the mentally ill. Other categories are eligible but in practice are automatically exempted: members of the Armed Forces, MPs, peers of the realm, doctors, nurses and others in the medical field.

No one with a serious criminal record is supposed to sit on a jury. Anyone who has had imposed on him a sentence of imprisonment (even if the sentence has been suspended) or community service within the previous ten years is disqualified, as are those who, within the past five years, have been given probation.

Anyone can ask to be excused from jury service because of particular personal circumstances: a blind, deaf or severely disabled person, for instance (though in 1999 a deaf man who wanted to serve on a jury was not allowed to, because he needed a sign language interpreter and this would have meant a thirteenth person in the jury room, which is forbidden). Mothers with very small children are usually excused; so are people running one-man businesses. A lot depends on the officials at the particular court. Some will allow people off jury service if it interferes with a planned holiday: others are more strict.

Home Office research in 1999 concluded startlingly that only one out of three people summoned for jury service actually turned up to do it. Some of those who didn't fell into the automatically exempt categories mentioned above, but nearly 40 per cent of those who didn't serve were excused for personal – mainly medical or work – reasons. There's a strong suspicion, backed by a lot of anecdotal evidence, that articulate middle-class and professional people can too easily escape jury service by writing persuasive, well-expressed letters giving spurious or dishonest reasons. The courts do not have the resources or time to check the veracity of requests pleading to be excused.

To speak of a random jury when so many categories of people are excluded and so many individuals can get off is unrealistic. A typical jury today is likely to be much younger, have a closer ratio of women to men, and have more working-class members than one of a quarter century ago – and more unemployed people. This is not to everyone's liking. The first objection is to the lower 18-year-old limit. A former Chief Constable put it this way:

I believe quite sincerely that 18 is far too young an age to select a juror. Yes, I know they can go in the army and fight for their country at 18. Yes, I know they've got the vote at 18. But quite honestly I do believe that at 18 a youngster has been protected by his parents or by his school or by his university; he hasn't yet had the chance to go out and earn his living and face all the trauma that entails, and I believe he's immature to the degree that he is not capable of giving a mature judgement on a set of facts pro and con, placed before him in a courtroom.

Some judges and barristers take the view that the lower age limit should be 25. Lord Denning's criticism took a different line, in *What Next in the Law* (Butterworths, 1982):

Nowadays virtually every member of the population is qualified to sit as a juror. No matter how illiterate or uneducated or unsuitable he may be. And where the chances, by sheer weight of numbers, are loaded heavily against the jurors being the sensible and responsible members of the community . . . There should be a qualification for service as a juror so that a jury is composed of sensible and responsible members of the community. It should be representative of the best of them . . .

The point often made about today's juries – forcefully, in 1999, by the former appeal court judge Sir Frederick Lawton – is that their level of understanding of cases, and perhaps their level of intelligence, are not always up to the task they have to perform. There is no educational qualification. There is not even a language or comprehension requirement to ensure that jurors who are called up at least understand the cases they have to try.

A jury panel is finally assembled at the court. How many are summoned will depend on the particular court they've been called to. The Old Bailey, with 18 courts normally sitting at one time, has between 300 and 350 jurors on the premises on any given day, both sitting on cases and waiting around. Smaller courthouses gear their numbers to their needs. The long uncomfortable wait begins. It is a recurring criticism of the system that it pays too little regard to jurors' comfort and does too little to tell them what is going on, although there is now a video shown to them about their role and duties. Eventually a batch of jurors is called to a particular court, but it will not necessarily be the first 12 who become the jury.

Until 1989 the law tolerated another assault on the principle of randomness, which occasionally resulted in unbalanced and unrepresentative juries and – some claimed and others denied – allowed guilty criminals to be wrongly acquitted. Every defendant had been entitled to three 'peremptory challenges' – the right to reject three potential jurors without giving any reasons. It did not matter too much when there was only one defendant, but when there were several co-accused and each had three challenges, the composition of the jury could be materially affected. So, for instance, challenges could be used to get rid of anyone who looked vaguely respectable or establishment, or was on the elderly side, or wore a tie, in the hope that the jurors who were left would be more likely to acquit.

The defendant's right of peremptory challenge was abolished in

1989. But the prosecution's equivalent right remains. The procedure is different, but the result is the same. Prosecuting counsel calls on a juror to 'stand by for the Crown', which means he goes to the back of the queue of potential jurors and in effect is never called again. In practice the prosecution's right to challenge in this way is used extremely rarely.

Both prosecution and defence also have an unlimited right to challenge for cause – to reject a juror for a particular reason. But this can create potential problems. How is the defence, in particular, to know whether there is something about the juror that justifies a challenge? In the USA a juror can be questioned at length about his beliefs and prejudices, sometimes in the full glare of the television cameras. Psychiatrists can be employed to assess potential jurors, and private detectives to rummage around their neighbourhood and workplace. In the trial of black activist Bobby Seale in 1971, no fewer than 1035 jurors were rejected before the final 12 were selected. The process took four months.

All this is foreign to the English system, though a judge can ask questions of a jury panel to make sure that none of them has a special link with the case – like knowing the accused. In the prosecution of Kevin and Ian Maxwell for fraud, for instance, questions were asked to make sure that no one with a link to Mirror Group Newspapers – whose pension fund was at the heart of the case – was on the jury.

The 12 who finally emerge from the selection process are now sworn. They promise: 'I will faithfully try the several issues joined between our sovereign lady the Queen and the prisoner at the Bar, and give a true verdict according to the evidence.'

The trial begins. The jury sit through, in silence, the speeches, the evidence, the cross-examination and finally, the judge's summing-up, which is specifically addressed to them. They do not interrupt much and seldom ask questions, although they are entitled to do so if they wish something to be clarified. They can take notes if they want to. The jury are given some of the documents in the case, but not necessarily all of them. The judge, at the end of his summing-up, emphasizes that the jury must try to reach a unanimous verdict. If they find they cannot reach a 12–0 decision, the judge may, after giving them an opportunity to agree, call them back and tell them he will accept a majority verdict of ten–two, or eleven–one. How long a judge will wait before telling them about the majority verdict depends on the complexity of the case, but it must not be less than two hours. It could be several hours, or even a day.

What actually happens in a jury room is supposed to be a secret, and the Contempt of Court Act 1981 makes it very difficult to find out. It is unlawful for a juror to reveal the secrets of the discussion in the jury room, or for a newspaper or anyone else to try to get the information by interviewing a juror. In 1992 the *Mail on Sunday* was found guilty of contempt of court and fined £75,000 for publishing interviews with jurors in the Blue Arrow fraud trial, in which they revealed how and why they had reached their verdicts.

But we do have some idea how juries operate. Several jurors wrote about their experiences before it was forbidden, and many others have talked about them. There have also been research studies, using 'shadow' juries, made up of ordinary members of the public who have been chosen in the normal way, attended a real case and then pretended to be the real jury. Their discussions were observed and noted by researchers. (And of course there is the film *Twelve Angry Men*, which for anyone who has not been on a jury is probably the main, though highly misleading, reference point for what goes on when a jury retires.)

Our information is therefore mainly anecdotal, with old academic research a secondary source. For many years there has been a campaign led by lawyers and academics to allow research into how juries reached their decisions, the better to know how well the system actually worked. Such research would not name jurors or identify cases, and individual jurors would still be banned from publicly revealing their experiences in specific trials, especially high-profile ones. The government has shown occasional signs of agreeing to open up jury research for academic purposes, but legislation on the subject is not imminent.

Not surprisingly, the anecdotes told about jury experiences are many and varied and there is a vast division of opinion about the system. Horrific tales are related of the inability of jurors to understand the most basic points, of their total silence throughout, of a bully's hectoring the others into submission, of a pressing dinner engagement determining which way a juror voted, and of sheer prejudice – against blacks, policemen, the Irish or the young. A woman juror in Croydon managed to get taken off the jury altogether when she revealed that she was extremely racially prejudiced. But there will be just as many stories about how conscientiously a jury debated the issues, how closely they followed the evidence, how much time they devoted to sifting each detail, how they stuck to the facts and refused to make assumptions based on prejudice. *The Juryman's Tale* by Trevor Grove (Bloomsbury, 2000) is an interesting inside look at the system from the point of view of a juror.

The truth about juries is that, like judges and magistrates, there are some very good ones and some bad ones, just as one would expect from such a random exercise. There will inevitably be some people who play a bigger part in the discussion than others, some who will understand the legal nuances and the facts better, some who will tend to believe the police and others who will be much more defence-minded, some who will be more patient than others. But there is very little evidence, anecdotal or otherwise, to suggest that there is anything fundamentally unsatisfactory in the way juries reach their verdicts.

Different juries approach their task in different ways, even from the very first decision – choosing one of them as foreman or fore-woman. There are no set rules, so the jury muddle through as best they can. Some juries pick someone among them who, by dress, accent or general appearance, seems (rightly or wrongly) competent at running things. Others prefer to go for someone who has been on a jury before, and therefore is assumed to know the ropes. Or it may be done by names in a hat, or volunteering. Nor are there any set rules for the foreman. He can conduct the discussion in whatever way he thinks best, from a formal chairman approach to a free-for-all.

The way juries approach a case is often equally unsystematic. Philip Sealy of the London School of Economics studied some hundreds of shadow juries during the 1970s. He found that juries did not necessarily work through the evidence systematically in the order it was given. They did not always discuss the burden of proof – the presumption of innocence – which is at the heart of the system. They did not always fully understand the legal distinctions explained to them (between dangerous and careless driving in Smith's case, for instance). But in the end, they usually got the facts right and they often reached the right result according to the law, even if they had imperfectly understood it.

What matters is not so much that every member of the jury should understand every nuance of the law and every factual detail, but that they should in the end use their collective commonsense to reach a correct conclusion.

The crucial question is whether or not they get it right. It is not easy to tell. People who are wrongly acquitted are hardly likely to advertise the jury's mistake. The police believe that juries often do acquit the guilty, but this is not necessarily a point against the jury: it may be because the police have badly prepared, or the prosecution badly presented, the case, or there has been a technicality to do with the evidence. Nor can we assess how often juries wrongly convict from the number of successful appeals against their verdicts. Because juries never give reasons for their decisions, it is often very difficult to find a ground of appeal. Unless there is new evidence, the only way to upset a jury's verdict is to find something wrong with the trial itself, for instance, an irregularity in the proceedings, or the judge's misleading summing-up, or evidence allowed in that should have been ruled inadmissible. It is impossible to go behind a jury's verdict and it is not enough for an appellant just to claim that the jury were wrong. It is quite possible, perhaps probable, that juries have mistakenly convicted people where no appeal was possible because no specific ground for appeal could be found.

In 1977 two legal academics, John Baldwin and Michael McConville, conducted a survey to try to assess how many wrongful verdicts juries reached. They looked at 370 trials in Birmingham and spoke to the trial judge, prosecution and defence counsel, and often the police officer in charge of the case. They compared the views of those participants with the actual verdicts reached. For the most part they tallied, but in a surprisingly large number of cases – 15 per cent – the trial judge and at least one other party disagreed with the jury's conclusion. This does not of course necessarily mean that the jury was wrong and the judge always right. In most cases where other participants in the trial disagreed with the jury's verdict, the judge would have convicted where the jury decided the defendant was not guilty. But in some cases it was the other way around. The jury found the defendant guilty when the judge, and sometimes even the police officer, would have acquitted. Even making all allowances, that survey suggests that if the Birmingham figures are applied throughout the country, hundreds of people are being wrongly convicted by juries every year. That in itself does not necessarily damn the jury system. Would the number of wrongful convictions be fewer under any other system? Would judges sitting on their own make fewer mistakes? It's impossible to tell. But no criminal justice process in the world can ever be foolproof.

If we believe the jury system to be inadequate, what are we to put in its place? Professor Hogan argued that juries were being asked to do something which is essentially a professional task:

To find facts, and – this is more important – draw the appropriate inferences from fact. I believe those matters to call for professional skills and professional judgement, which the jury does not have.

The judge tells us the story of the case, he finds the facts. He says which persons he believed, which persons he did not believe, and he puts the story together, and he draws the appropriate inferences . . . The convicted accused in the criminal case would know why he had been convicted, what was regarded as important and what was regarded as unimportant. He would be, so far as an appeal is concerned, in a stronger position.

Such views have their supporters, but those who would wish to abolish the jury altogether are still in a small minority and there is no agreement about how to replace it. Defenders of the jury system say that the judge would become too case-hardened, that he would be unable to take a fresh look at every case before him. A jury, by contrast, have none of the preconceptions born of too many years doing the same job.

Perhaps more importantly, juries have a value above that of the verdicts they deliver. They are the direct link between the ordinary person and the administration of justice. The jury system provides a vital element of community participation in the workings of our society. It is a necessary reassurance that justice is not meted out by a remote élite but is something in which every citizen in a democratic society can play a part.

Juries are important, too, as a barometer of public feeling on the state of the law. They can and do express their displeasure about a particular law or a particular prosecution by refusing to convict, as they did when Clive Ponting was prosecuted under the Official Secrets Act for leaking information about the background to the Falklands War – the jury acquitted in spite of the judge telling them he had no defence – or when they acquitted two men, Randle and Pottle, accused of helping the Soviet spy George Blake escape in 1966, because they clearly felt that a prosecution should not have been brought 26 years after the event. It is mainly because juries were refusing to convict publishers charged with publishing obscene books that the law has all but fallen into disuse.

In the past their role has been even more dramatic. In the latter days of the death penalty in Britain they were often reluctant to convict of murder, even when the facts bore out the charge, because of a likelihood that the accused, for whom they might have had some sympathy, would be hanged. Even longer ago, it was the refusal of juries to find defendants guilty of sheep stealing which caused it to be removed from the list of capital crimes. Lord Elwyn-Jones, a former Lord Chancellor, commented:

The value of the jury in protecting the citizen in that way and in putting some control over the power of the executive to impose and try to inflict unjust criminal laws on the community, the presence of those 12 men and women – the palladium of our liberty – to decide his fate ultimately is very important.

It is arguable, however, that this function is no longer as important as it used to be. Our laws are less stringent than they were, our fundamental civil liberties are not as much under attack, and when they are, there are other bodies to defend them.

One issue in particular has given rise to controversy. Many argue that a jury is not an appropriate body for determining guilt or innocence in long and complicated fraud trials, or other cases which require the detailed inspection of accounts and figures. First, such cases tend to be inordinately long – often several months or even, as in the Blue Arrow case or the prosecution of a fraud relating to an amusement park in Nottingham, more than a year. Second, they require a high degree of numeracy and financial understanding from a jury which is not chosen with those qualities in mind. Often the accountants and the financial experts are at odds about the figures, and the judge is frequently at sixes and sevens – how can a jury of ordinary men and women possibly cope? A further point is that jurors who have the time to sit for several months cannot be typical, or the jury in any way random.

The Fraud Trials Committee, under the chairmanship of Lord Roskill, a law lord, agreed with these points. In a report published in 1986, the Committee proposed that in especially complex fraud trials the jury should be replaced by a judge and two lay members with knowledge and experience of financial dealings. The government rejected that proposal. Lawyers and judges are not unanimous. Supporters of retaining juries claim that there is no evidence that fraud juries do not know what is happening. Anyway, they don't really decide financial issues: their job, as in every other criminal case, is usually to decide whom to believe, who's telling the truth – a task for which juries are well suited. Although the debate over the suitability of juries for fraud trials continues, the government shows no signs of taking steps to abolish them.

For the foreseeable future, the jury system is firmly entrenched. It may be the subject of further calls for reform, perhaps on the need for some sort of language or comprehension test for jurors. It may be tinkered with – or restricted, as the Home Secretary has been trying to do in removing the right to jury trial from some defendants (see p. 20) – but it is a reasonably safe bet that it will be there, more or less as we know it today, for a long time.

## The sentence

A trial is not always successful drama. Its structure often demands an anti-climax. The curtain falls on the second act with a dramatic exit line from the jury: their verdict of guilty or not guilty. (In practice, even this is messy – there are often many charges and several defendants to get through and the verdict-taking can last several minutes.) But the play only ends there if the accused has been acquitted. The final curtain can then descend amid scenes of joyful tears and jubilation. If the verdict is guilty, the actors have to play another act – the sentence.

The sentencing process does not take place only after a full-blown trial. Most accused – 70 per cent at the Crown Court – plead guilty. When there has been a trial the judge and the public will know all the evidence, in detail. With a guilty plea, however, nothing is known except the bald charge, and in those cases prosecution counsel will give a short outline of the main facts of the offence. No witnesses are called. From then on the procedure is the same as with conviction by a jury.

First, the prosecution provides the judge with information about the accused's previous criminal record, if he has one, including whether he is already on probation or under a suspended sentence for a previous offence. The document containing his criminal record will also give brief details of his education, employment and home circumstances – 'evidence of character', as it is called. John Smith has one previous motoring conviction, for speeding. He was fined £50 and his licence was endorsed with three penalty points.

Next, a pre-sentence report may be submitted, especially where there's the prospect of the accused being sent to prison. This is a comprehensive inquiry, prepared by a probation officer, on the defendant's background, family, home circumstances, relationships, attitudes, job situation and prospects. The report is based on interviews with the accused and those who know him well. If the accused has pleaded guilty, he may have explained his motives to the probation officer. The report usually concludes with the probation officer's opinion on the subject's suitability or otherwise for a non-prison sentence. It may suggest, for instance, that he would respond positively to probation or community service, or it may conclude that his attitude is unlikely to make these methods successful.

There may also be medical or psychiatric reports given to the judge, where the accused's mental state may be relevant to the reasons for committing the crime or to the sentence about to be imposed. Sometimes, a 'character witness' is called to tell the judge, for instance, what an excellent person the accused is, and how out of character his crime was.

None of this applies to John Smith. There is no real likelihood of imprisonment and his crime is not the kind which requires reports.

Finally there is the plea in mitigation, delivered by the defendant's counsel (or the defendant himself if he is unrepresented). This is the tear-jerking speech of the last act, where the accused's barrister has the chance to plead for mercy and justice, to stress that the crime was the responsibility of society and not his client; alternatively, that he was led astray by evil companions. He produces a pregnant girlfriend whom the accused wants to marry and settle down with, and who will stick by him through thick and thin, and an employer who has offered him a job and is prepared to trust him. He exaggerates the remorse felt by his client and the enthusiasm with which he will reform.

Such eloquence is not necessary in John Smith's case. What Mr Brown stresses above all is how much Smith's job depends on keeping his driving licence. For Smith it is not so much the size of the fine that concerns him, but whether or not he will be able to carry on driving. Although judges and magistrates seldom disqualify someone convicted of mere careless driving, Mr Brown is taking no chances:

MR BROWN: He's a man whose job depends very much on his being able to drive. He covers a very high annual mileage, some 40,000 miles according to my instructions. And Your Honour may think that it's very much to his credit that he has only that one endorsement on his licence. Your Honour, he's 36 years of age; he's been driving for many years. Your Honour may think that it would be very difficult for this man, who's been a salesman all his working life, to obtain alternative employment, were he to lose his licence. That would be the position, in my respectful submission. If he loses his licence, he loses his livelihood and you see how much his employers think of him. [A letter from Smith's employer has been handed in to the judge.] Your Honour, I hope that the court will feel that in the particular circumstances of this case, that is, not only the circumstances of the accident, but the defendant's own personal circumstances, it will not be necessary to disqualify him.

The judge now has all the information on which to base his decision. The time has come for what is for many defendants the most heart-stopping moment of all, the sentence itself. This is what the training of judges is mainly aimed at; they learn the range of sentences they can apply, and the factors they should take into account. In the majority of cases the accused will know more or less what he can expect. He will have been told by his lawyers what the maximum penalty is but also that he can expect far less than that maximum. The top of the scale would only be imposed for the most heinous possible version of the crime. The maximum for theft, for instance, is seven years' imprisonment, but only a tiny percentage would get even half that – and they would be thieves with very long records. This is typical of many categories of offence. Murder is unique in having a fixed mandatory penalty, life imprisonment, although this does not usually mean life: some murderers – the women who kill their husbands after years of brutal treatment, or mercy killers – may be released after a few years. A policeman's killer will stay in for 20 or 30; some murderers, like Myra Hindley, may stay in literally for the rest of their lives.

There is a 'tariff' for most kinds of offence. It is not an exact number of years or an exact amount of money, but it is a range within which judges tend to stay. It is not laid down by law but is the distillation of the collective practice of the courts, supported by guidance from the Lord Chief Justice and from judgments of the Court of Appeal in cases that have come before it. So, for example, judges know that for a rape a sentence of at least five years is appropriate. If more than one attacker is involved, or there have been aggravating circumstances such as breaking into a house to commit the rape, or where the rapist is in a position of responsibility towards the victim, eight years is nearer the mark. Campaigns of rape which terrorize the public can fetch 15 years' imprisonment.

These are guidelines, and the judge will look at the actual circumstances before deciding on the exact sentence. Only if he finds highly exceptional circumstances, either in favour of or against the accused, will he normally stray from the framework laid down. If he is too lenient he will have to answer to the cry of public opinion and may receive a rap over the knuckles by the Lord Chancellor, as happened to the judge who sentenced a rapist to only a £2000 fine.

In 1989, mainly as a result of the public outcry following lenient sentences imposed on two men convicted of a violent and vicious rape on a young virgin at a vicarage in Ealing, London, the law was changed to allow, for the first time, appeals to the Court of Appeal against over-lenient sentences. Only the Attorney General can appeal, if he thinks that there are grounds for concern that a particular sentence is far too low. There have been several hundred such appeals since 1989, the vast majority successful in that the Appeal Court has increased the sentence. In 1998, 84 per cent of the 95 appeals resulted in higher sentences. The main categories of crime involved in appeals against leniency have been robbery, rape, causing grievous bodily harm, and causing death by driving. Highly publicized cases have included that of a 15-year-old boy, who was not sentenced to any form of detention for raping a 14-year-old girl, but where the judge insultingly ordered that the boy pay his victim £500 so that she could go on holiday; and a young man convicted of sexually abusing an eight-year-old girl, where the judge said that the victim 'was no angel' and didn't send the abuser to jail. In both cases the Court of Appeal substituted a custodial sentence on the offenders.

Similarly, tariffs are used at the other end of the criminal scale. There are regular detailed guidelines on the sentences to be imposed for various motoring (and other) offences. The rule of thumb for speeding, for instance, is that where the speed is less than 15 miles per hour above a 40 miles an hour speed limit, the fine on a driver of average income should be around £150; but if it's 30 miles an hour above, the fine is more than doubled and the penalty points rise as well. From 2000, there have also been guidelines – not firm tariffs – on how to impose fines on people of varying incomes. It is thought right that a well-off defendant should be paying a higher fine for the same offence than a poor one. The guidelines divide defendants into income bands, suggesting the appropriate fine for the particular offence within each band. The Magistrates' Courts guidelines also deal with more serious offences. For example, they suggest that house burglars should normally go to prison, but it would be a mitigating factor if the burglary was in the daytime, with no forcible entry, no one in the house, no damage done and not much stolen. In that case the burglar would probably escape jail. But if the crime was committed at night, and people inside were frightened, and it had been carefully planned and the burglars left a mess, then it would count very much against a non-custodial sentence. In addition, factors such as the degree of remorse shown by the accused, his co-operation with the police, his age and his mental or physical health would also be taken into account.

John Smith is sure that he will not go to prison. He expects a fine. But the important thing to him is what happens to his licence.

The judge considers the other information he has been given. He knows the accused's previous criminal record – obviously a clean sheet will incline him more favourably than a string of previous convictions, especially for similar offences. He will weigh the information in the pre-sentence report and other reports and assess the plea in mitigation. According to Gilbert and Sullivan's *The Mikado*, a judge's task is to let the punishment fit the crime, but nowadays this is only one aspect. The punishment (or treatment) must also fit the offender.

The judge's first important task is to decide whether or not to send the accused to prison. For the defendant this is a crucial issue. It is now generally accepted by everyone in the criminal justice system that imprisoning an offender for the first time can have drastic consequences, not just for the criminal, but for his family as well; and that the benefits to society of imposing a custodial sentence are not always clear-cut. In addition, some of our prisons are overcrowded to an extent that even the government admits has resulted in unacceptable, degrading and inhumane conditions.

As a result, the law tells the judge always to ask himself whether the crime is so serious that no sentence other than imprisonment will do.

If a judge decides that there is no alternative to prison, the question is: for how long? Apart from the tariff and the factors particular to the individual, the judge must also consider his public duty. Is it the sort of crime that needs a long period of custody to protect the public from the offender, even if there are mitigating personal factors? Is a deterrent sentence necessary, aimed not so much at the defendant himself but at others who might be tempted to commit similar offences? Criminologists have argued mightily over whether or not deterrent sentences have any effect. The stiff sentences passed on whites found guilty of beating up blacks in Notting Hill in 1958 are believed to have had immediate deterrent effect, but the generality of the proposition is not universally accepted.

The judge must also bear in mind guidelines from successive Lord Chief Justices, backed by Lord Chancellors and Home Secretaries, and many others, to consider passing shorter rather than longer sentences on a wide range of offenders. Such a policy would not apply to criminals convicted of offences involving violence, or to others who are a real menace to society. It has come to be realized, however, that for many offenders, especially first-timers, the main effect of imprisonment is often achieved in the initial stages of the sentence. A much longer term is counter-productive. It only accustoms the prisoner to incarceration, and hardens and embitters him. A one-month sentence can be more effective than three months, and, further up the scale, 12 months can be as productive as 18 months or two years.

For John Smith the moment has come. The sentence is pronounced, usually with a few accompanying remarks revealing the main factors which weighed in the judge's mind. But the judge rarely gives elaborate reasons, and often he will say very little. In John Smith's case he has only this to say:

*JUDGE*: This case can be summed up, as far as you're concerned, that on that unfortunate day, you drove at a greatly excessive speed and you were therefore quite unable to control your vehicle in an emergency, whether there was a motor-cycle there or not.

But for Smith, the important words are these:

In order to relieve your worries, may I say at once that I don't intend to
disqualify you from driving, having regard to what Mr Brown has ably said
on your behalf. This case is going to be met with a fine, and the fine in your
case will be one of £400.

His licence is endorsed with six penalty points.

The trial is over. If the accused has been sentenced to imprisonment,
he descends for the last time from the dock to the cells below, there
to wait to be taken to start his period of imprisonment. If he has been
in custody during the trial, even if he is not given a sentence of
imprisonment, or even if he is acquitted, he will probably have to go
down anyway, to go through the formalities of release. John Smith has
no such formalities to go through. He can leave the court immediately.
Within minutes the courtroom is empty.

## Main types of sentence

*Absolute discharge*: no financial penalty, no conditions.

*Conditional discharge*: no financial penalty, but if offender commits
similar crime in stated period (12 months, say) can be brought back
and given a more severe sentence for the original offence.

*Fine*: up to £5000 at magistrates' court, unlimited in the Crown Court.

*Probation order*: offender placed under the supervision of a probation
officer for specified period (often one or two years). Has to have
regular contact with him. Other conditions can be attached, such
as that offender must take medical treatment.

*Community service order*: expressed in hours (between 40 and 240).
Offender carries out socially useful tasks, such as helping with the
disabled, or decorating elderly people's houses, at weekends and
other spare time.

*Suspended sentence of imprisonment*: for example 'nine months suspended for two years'. If offender commits another offence within
the stated period, the original sentence can (at the discretion of
judge or magistrate) be activated, and he can be made to serve it
after any sentence imposed for the subsequent offence.

*Imprisonment*: the offender goes to prison – but for how long does he stay there? The sentence imposed by the judge – to the anger of critics – is almost never the real length of incarceration. If sentenced to less than a year, the offender is released after serving one-half the sentence. If the sentence is between one and four years, he's released under supervision after one-half served; and could be subject to conditions on release. Longer-term prisoners – sentenced to four years or more – may be released after half their term, if they apply to the Parole Board and the Board recommends it (though the Home Secretary has the final say). If they're not released earlier, they have to be let out after two-thirds of the sentence. There is then a period on licence. If they're in breach of the licence, e.g. they re-offend or don't keep to the conditions, it can mean a recall to prison. The judge has an obligation to explain clearly what the sentence means in real terms – how long the accused will actually have to spend inside.

In 1997 a new draconian and controversial sentence came into effect. An offender who has already been convicted of a serious offence (like rape or robbery) will get an automatic sentence of life imprisonment if he commits another serious offence. This is familiarly known as the 'two strikes and you're out' rule.

Sentencing policy for adults seldom remains consistent and coherent for very long. The fashion, until recently, was to punish serious criminals with heavy sentences – where there has been violence, sexual assault, offences against children, drug dealing, or the public needs to be protected – but to try as far as possible to keep lesser criminals out of jail. The emphasis in the late 1980s and early 1990s was to promote 'community sentences' – what used to be referred to as 'non-custodial' – not as some soft option akin to getting away with it, but as tough punishments in their own right, albeit in the community rather than in prison. Then came another switch, back towards imprisonment, with the Conservative Home Secretary, Michael Howard, leading the way with his slogan 'Prison Works'. The Labour Home Secretary, Jack Straw, while not adopting that slogan, has taken a tough line on criminals, with imprisonment playing a central role. The judges who have to impose the sentences have expressed their unhappiness with some of the new rules they're having to follow, especially those which remove their discretion and make them impose mandatory sentences, like the 'two strikes' rule.

The range of sentences for a young offender – under 18 – is slightly different. To try to nip a potential criminal career in the bud, a 1999 Act of Parliament will allow magistrates to refer first-time offenders to a special youth panel which will look into the background of his offending and draw up a contract with the young delinquent and his parents, aimed at dealing with the root causes of his behaviour. If the contract – which could include the offender making reparations and apologizing to his victim – is kept to, there will be no further court appearance.

There is a sliding scale of penalties that can be imposed at different ages. Below 14 he can be absolutely or conditionally discharged, fined (and his parent(s) made liable if he doesn't pay), ordered to spend time at an attendance centre (where he spends several hours, often on successive Saturday afternoons, doing supervised recreational activities) or given a supervision order, under which he is supervised by a probation officer and may have to meet conditions laid down about where he lives and what he does.

Children under 14 who have committed murder (like those who killed the toddler James Bulger) are detained in custody 'at Her Majesty's pleasure' – the equivalent of life imprisonment for an adult.

At 14 a young offender can be detained for certain other serious crimes (in addition to murder and manslaughter), like robbery. Only when he reaches 15 can the court sentence him to detention in a young offender institution, for up to two years, for a wide range of criminality. At 16 he graduates to being liable for probation, the adult form of a supervision order, and for community service.

Since 1998 persistent young offenders – out-of-control tearaways responsible for dozens, sometimes hundreds, of offences – can be given a 'detention and training order'. This power can, in theory, be used to keep children as young as ten in some form of secure accommodation, for the protection of the public.

## Plea-bargaining

An accused has the right to change his plea from not guilty to guilty whenever he wants, before or even during his trial. He may do so, often on the advice of his lawyer, because it is generally true that the sentence will be lower on a guilty plea than if he fights the case to the end and is convicted. The judge gives a 'discount' for the fact that the accused saved the court's time (and public money) and spared witnesses from having to give evidence. Sometimes an accused will change his plea because of a bargain struck between the defence and prosecution barristers, often with the approval of the judge. Where, for instance, there are alternative charges against the accused, one more serious than the other (murder and manslaughter, or assault occasioning grievous bodily harm reduced to a less serious form of assault are examples), the prosecution may offer to drop the more serious charge if the accused pleads guilty to the lesser.

Even where there is only one charge, the judge sometimes lets it be known, informally, to the defence barrister, that if the defendant changes his plea to guilty, he will not pass a sentence of imprisonment. The judge will not specifically say that he will definitely imprison the defendant if he persists in pleading not guilty and is convicted, but the implication is well understood.

The advantage of plea-bargaining is that the accused (assuming he is guilty) can minimize the sentence, the prosecution still get their conviction, and cases take far less time. It is clearly also an advantage to know what is in the judge's mind. Critics of plea-bargaining point to the risk that the accused is put under great pressure to plead guilty to a charge that he really wants to fight. There have been cases of innocent defendants pleading guilty to get the case over with, once the threat of imprisonment has been removed by the plea bargain. The Court of Appeal has laid down that the accused must remain free to make up his own mind, but he sometimes finds it difficult to resist his own lawyer's offer. The pressure on him is the stronger because he is in the dark about what actually takes place between the judge and the barristers. The accused himself, the subject of the bargain, is excluded from the negotiations about it.

# Trials in magistrates' courts

Why do some defendants choose trial by jury rather than by the justices? First, a jury is far more likely to acquit than magistrates, especially in motoring cases. Most members of a jury know that they have themselves committed the odd motoring offence. They can identify with a defendant and are likely to be more sympathetic to his defence. Magistrates claim that their higher conviction rate means only that they are less gullible. They vehemently reject the implication that they convict more innocent people. They do not mind agreeing that they may convict a larger proportion of guilty offenders than juries do.

Second, a defendant will not necessarily get legal aid for a lawyer to defend him in the magistrates' court. Many, though not all, lower courts are very reluctant to give legal aid in motoring cases, while virtually all defendants pleading not guilty in the Crown Court, whatever they are charged with, are likely to get legal aid.

A third reason for going to the Crown Court is that if any legal issues are involved, on the admissibility of evidence for instance, a judge is more likely to deal with them expertly and correctly than magistrates, even with the help of their clerk.

In contrast, there are a number of advantages of trial by magistrates. First, cases do not take as long to come to trial. Waiting for trial creates understandable tensions and anxieties, and many defendants want nothing more than to have the case behind them as soon as possible. Second, cases themselves take less time. Third, the atmosphere in a magistrates' court is far less intimidating than in a Crown Court. Finally, though importantly, magistrates' justice is far cheaper. A one-day trial in a magistrates' court, with a barrister, might cost a few hundred pounds; at the Crown Court the trial would take two days and probably cost many thousands.

The object of the trial in the magistrates' court is exactly the same as in the Crown Court: to reach a verdict of guilty or not guilty and, if the result is a conviction, to pass sentence on the offender. The burden of proof on the prosecution and the rules of evidence apply equally to both kinds of court. The procedure, too, is broadly the same. But the absence of the jury and the relative triviality of the charges in the magistrates' court make a considerable difference to the spectacle. Instead of a bewigged judge in colourful robes sitting in solitary splendour, there are three ordinary-looking men and women wearing their ordinary clothes, neither wigged nor gowned.

The magistrates have the function of both judge and jury. They control the case, rule on points of law (with the help of their clerk), reach a decision and pass sentence. The trial follows the same path as its Crown Court equivalent. After the charge and the plea of not guilty, the prosecutor makes an opening speech, though it is addressed of course to the magistrates and not to a jury. He examines the witnesses, who are then cross-examined by the defence. At the end of the prosecution case, the defence lawyer has the chance to make his submission that there is no case to answer. If that fails, he calls his witnesses, usually including the accused, who are in turn cross-examined by the prosecution. In the magistrates' court the prosecution do not always have a second, closing, speech. The defence do, however, address the magistrates at the end of their case. There is of course no equivalent of the judge's summing-up.

A magistrates' decision need not be unanimous – a two to one majority will do. Some stipendiary magistrates give reasons for their findings, but lay justices rarely do, an omission which has been the subject of criticism. Perhaps they are bearing in mind the advice of Lord Mansfield, a former Lord Chief Justice:

Consider what you think justice requires and decide accordingly. But never give your reasons; for your judgment will probably be right but your reasons will certainly be wrong.

If the magistrates convict, the procedure for sentencing is much the same as in a Crown Court.

# Appeals

It is inevitable that the two million or so criminal cases a year in England and Wales should lead to a burning sense of injustice in a few thousand hearts. Some cope with it by trying to put it behind them, forgetting the ghastly experience rather than allowing it to continue to dominate their lives. For others, the system of appeals offers some, though not perfect, relief from what they regard as injustice.

There are two main springboards for appeal: the conviction and the sentence. The two are fundamentally different. In the first the appellant claims that the result was wrong, that he was innocent of the crime of which he was found guilty. If his contention is right, and if it is true of many convicted defendants, then it is a large blot on our system of justice, quite apart from the incalculable effect that every individual injustice has on its victim. Of course there are degrees – a conviction for overstaying a parking meter when in fact the meter was faulty is unjust, but quickly forgotten; at the other extreme there are people who have spent many years in prison for crimes they have not committed, and there have in the past been men such as Timothy Evans who were hanged and later found to be innocent. The second kind of appeal, against sentence, has a different basis: 'I did it, but I didn't deserve such a severe sentence.' The injustice is there, but it is of a different kind.

Our system of appeals is deficient in one important respect, which is unfortunately a necessary corollary of our trial system. Magistrates very seldom give any reasons when they decide to convict a defendant. Nor do a jury when delivering their guilty verdict. We are not told, although of course we can often infer, why the decision was guilty or not guilty. Magistrates and juries do not reveal that they believed that witness or disbelieved this alibi, or thought that the defendant was shifty in the witness box. So appeals have to be founded on other grounds.

Appeals against convictions by magistrates are in the form of a complete re-hearing of the case before a Crown Court judge, sitting with (different) magistrates. The witnesses appear again and give their evidence again and the judge and justices then make up their minds according to the evidence they have heard. Where a point of law, rather than a difference about the facts, is involved there is also a form of appeal directly from magistrates' courts to the Divisional Court of the Queen's Bench Division. Appeals against magistrates' sentences also go to a Crown Court judge, sitting with magistrates.

A jury's verdict is more difficult to appeal against. They have left no clue as to their reasons. So the appeal against conviction – which goes to the Court of Appeal's Criminal Division – has to be based on other factors, for instance that there was an irregularity in the trial (in one case, for instance, the judge pressured a jury into reaching a premature verdict), or that the judge wrongly directed the jury in his summing-up, or made a wrong legal decision during the trial (like allowing in inadmissible evidence). Up to 1988, the Court of Appeal's power to order a retrial was limited to cases where fresh evidence had come to light. Now, however, it is able to send cases back for retrial in far wider circumstances.

Over the years, the Court of Appeal has been criticized for failing to correct cases of apparent miscarriage of justice by taking an unduly restrictive view of its role and placing, in practice, far too great a burden on the appellant to prove his innocence. In particular, the court has been attacked for being loath to accept that evidence unearthed since the trial might have influenced the jury towards acquittal if they had heard it. The appellant was also at a disadvantage because the court would usually not interfere with a guilty verdict on the grounds that his lawyer handled the case badly, or used wrong tactics. So if his counsel didn't, for tactical reasons, call a particular witness for the defence who could have been called, the accused was stuck with that decision.

The wave of miscarriages of justice revealed at the end of the 1980s and beginning of the 1990s – the Guildford Four, the Birmingham Six, the Maguire family, Judith Ward, Winston Silcott, the Darvell brothers, the Cardiff Three, Stefan Kiszko, the Taylor sisters, and many less prominent cases – showed clearly that the existing machinery for appealing against convictions was seriously flawed. The reasons for the injustices included straightforward misbehaviour by the police, dubious scientific evidence and the withholding from the defence of important facts which might have pointed to the accused's innocence. What they had in common was that the restrictive rules governing appeals, coupled with the uneasy passing-the-buck procedure between the Home Secretary and the appeal court, meant that innocent people had spent many unnecessary years in prison.

It was the release of the Birmingham Six in 1991 that led directly to the setting up of the Royal Commission on Criminal Justice, under the chairmanship of Lord Runciman. The Commission proposed a separate, independent authority to deal with alleged miscarriages of justice. The Criminal Cases Review Commission (CCRC), which has both lawyer and non-lawyer members, started work in 1997. It receives claims of wrongful convictions, initiates and supervises investigations into those claims, gathers the evidence together and decides whether or not to send the case to the Court of Appeal. In effect, it's a filter through which allegations of innocence are sifted. There is a general view that the CCRC does its work well, and it has brought many cases to the appeal court which have resulted in miscarriages of justice being put right. But it is inadequately funded and has a large backlog of cases waiting attention.

It is also injustice when guilty criminals go free, and there has been concern that the law doesn't permit the retrial of convicted defendants who have been let off on appeal because of a technicality, even where the evidence against them is very strong. Other defendants may have been acquitted at their trial, after which new evidence pointing to their guilt has come to light. Under the existing law, they can't be tried again, because of the doctrine that this would be 'double jeopardy'. Partly as a result of what was revealed in the inquiry into the death of Stephen Lawrence, the government's legal think-tank, the Law Commission, studied the issue and recommended that acquitted accused should have to face another trial if new evidence arose pointing firmly to their guilt – for example DNA tests which hadn't been available at the original trial. The government looks likely to bring those proposals into law.

Winning an appeal against sentence is not easy either. It is not enough that the appeal judges would have imposed a lower sentence.

They have to be convinced that the sentence actually imposed was unreasonably high.

Some appeals arising from criminal trials will go to the House of Lords, but only if they involve important legal points. The kind of issues that the law lords have tackled in recent years include: Should adults who participate in consensual sado-masochistic practices in private be subject to the criminal law? Can a husband be convicted of raping his wife while they are still living together? When should a person who isn't carrying a weapon be guilty of murder if his accomplice stabs someone to death?

Finally, the Attorney General is entitled to refer points of law to the Court of Appeal for clarification, even if the accused has been acquitted. The decisions in such cases do not affect the accused. An acquittal is not changed into a conviction if the Attorney General's point is ruled valid, but the Court of Appeal's decision will be a precedent for subsequent cases on the same point. The government is also looking into the possibility of giving the prosecution a right of appeal against a trial judge's decision on a legal point which has the effect of stopping the trial – for example, if the judge rules that an important bit of evidence is not admissible, and the trial folds as a result, the prosecution ought to have the right to challenge that ruling on appeal.

## The future

In 1999 the Lord Chancellor announced a comprehensive review of the entire process in the criminal courts, to be conducted by a senior appeal court judge, Lord Justice Auld. In particular, the review will be aimed at making the process more efficient and reducing the unacceptable delays. The judge is expected to report in early 2001.

# Criminal justice and human rights

The European Convention on Human Rights, which becomes part of national law on 2 October 2000 (under the Human Rights Act), says that everyone is 'entitled to a fair and public hearing before an impartial tribunal' (Article 6). It is likely that a large number of challenges to the criminal justice system will be made, claiming a breach of that guarantee. The failure of magistrates to give reasons is expected to be one area of challenge – how can a convicted person properly exercise the right to appeal, unless the court has given its reasons? Claims under the Human Rights Act are expected to include allegations to do with judges' or magistrates' financial or personal interests, memberships of societies or strong opinions which made them less than impartial. Other claims might be based on the rules governing the prosecution's duty to disclose important evidence to the defence; the shifting of the 'burden of proof' so as to tamper with an accused's 'presumption of innocence'; and restrictions on the so-called right to silence.

## Adversarial v. inquisitorial

In the English adversarial, or accusatorial, system of trial, the day of the trial is crucial. This is when the two contestants, their training and preparation completed, climb into the ring. The result is always in doubt. One of the combatants may be favourite – it may seem like an open-and-shut case for the prosecution – but there is always the chance of an upset. Nothing can be taken for granted. No doubt such a system can produce tension, but does it deliver justice? In particular, does our trial system get at the truth? Or is it so much of a tactical game that sometimes truth and justice take second place?

In the English system the police and the prosecution build up a case against the accused. It is then left to the defence to demolish it. At no stage before the trial does any independent mind look at the case as a whole. All depends on what happens in court and sometimes important witnesses, who could give vital evidence, are not heard by the jury at all. Another aspect of the adversarial system is that – much as one would like to think that justice always triumphs – court battles can be won or lost by advocacy. A good barrister, both by his skill at questioning and cross-examination, and by his speeches to the jury, can sometimes turn a losing case into a 50/50 hope, and a finely balanced one into a winner. Juries are not as susceptible to flowing oratory and appeals to emotion as they used to be, and such tactics today could even prove counter-productive. But it is only human nature to be impressed by good advocacy. Experienced judges admit that advocacy can make a difference to the result, though only in a very small percentage of trials.

Few lawyers and judges deny the possibility that innocent men have been sent to prison because their advocates failed to rise to the occasion, and that criminals are walking free because of the excellence of their lawyers' presentation. Is it justice that the result of a trial should hinge purely on one side's having a better advocate than the other? Perhaps not, though it is probably inevitable under our system where so much depends on what happens in court.

These are question marks against the adversarial system. The alternative is the inquisitorial, which most other European countries have in one form or another. The details vary from country to country, but the French example demonstrates the essential elements of the system.

Far more investigations and inquiries are carried out before the trial, so that not as much depends on what happens at the trial itself. Under the French system, when a serious crime is committed, an examining magistrate (*juge d'instruction*) is appointed to look into it. He is a professional judge, usually relatively junior, whose job it is to decide whether a particular accused should be prosecuted. The strength of the French system lies in the thoroughness of the investigation of the crime, with the examining magistrate in overall control. His job is to find out as much as possible about the circumstances and background of the crime and of the person suspected of it. He is responsible for the police conduct of the investigation, and has the power himself to interrogate anyone whom he thinks can throw any light on the crime, including the suspect and any witnesses. He can even hold confrontations between the accused and witnesses. He arranges for all the necessary medical and psychiatric examinations of the accused, and all inquiries into his background. Eventually a full dossier is built up and the *juge d'instruction* is in a position to decide whether or not the prosecution should go ahead and on what charges.

After making his recommendation he drops out of the picture, and the case proceeds to trial, or the accused is set free.

The system is designed to uncover the truth by pre-trial inquisition, and the French examining magistrate's task is to get at the truth. It is as much his duty to find factors pointing to innocence as to seek out evidence of guilt.

There is a common belief that in France an accused is presumed guilty until proved innocent. That is untrue and misleading. What is true, however, is that because so much is done before trial to find out the truth, those who eventually appear before a court are more likely to be convicted, because inquiries have been so much more thorough than their English equivalent. In France more than 90 per cent who are tried for serious crimes are convicted. In England the figure is fewer than 40 per cent. But under the French system many are released at an early stage who in England would have to go through the trauma of a trial.

Which is the better system, the gladiatorial, allowing the two sides to choose their weapons, or the inexorably truth-seeking inquisitorial? The 1993 Royal Commission on Criminal Justice studied a number of 'inquisitorial' systems, but came to the conclusion that they were not necessarily better in reaching a just result. The Commission doubted

. . . whether the fusion of the functions of investigation and prosecution, and the direct involvement of judges in both, are more likely to serve the interests of justice than a system in which the roles of police, prosecutors and judges are as far as possible kept separate . . . We believe that a system in which the critical roles are kept separate offers a better protection for the innocent defendant, including protection against the risk of unnecessarily prolonged detention prior to trial.

# CHAPTER VII

# The Civil Process

The accident in which John Smith knocked down Anne Jones in his car has had dramatic consequences for both of them. Smith has had to face a criminal court. And, through no fault of her own, Anne Jones has suffered an injury. The accident has changed her life, not only causing continuing pain, but reducing her standard of living. Does the law offer her a remedy? Can someone be made to pay?

## Types of claim

John Smith has been prosecuted and found guilty by a criminal court. Careless driving is a crime for which the state can levy a punishment, in John Smith's case a fine. But in injuring Anne Jones he may also have committed a 'tort' – a civil wrong which injures someone or harms a person's property or reputation. If Anne Jones can prove that John Smith committed a tort against her – or if he admits it – she can claim compensation from him in the civil courts.

The tort involved in this case is negligence. Anne Jones will claim that John Smith caused her injury by failing to take the sort of care a reasonable driver would be expected to take. Negligence can occur in many other situations as well: for example, when a hospital gives a patient a transfusion of the wrong type of blood, or a solicitor gives his client wrong advice because he has overlooked a new law, or a company fails to make sure its employees' working conditions are safe, or a council fails to repair a loose paving stone. Anybody who is injured or who suffers financial loss through someone else's negligence has a right to sue in the civil courts for compensation.

Negligence is only one of a range of torts, or wrongs, for which it is possible to sue and claim damages. Other torts include assault, defamation (injuring someone else's reputation), and nuisance (spoiling someone else's enjoyment of his property, for example, by creating excessive noise or nasty smells). But by far the most common tort, in terms of the number of court actions started, is negligence.

Apart from tort, the other big category of civil action is for breach of contract. When two parties enter into a contract, they both agree to carry out certain obligations. For instance, if a householder asks a firm of builders to do some work on his house, he agrees to pay them and they agree to do the job in a workmanlike manner. If he refuses to pay, they can sue him. He can then put in a defence alleging shoddy workmanship, if this is his reason for refusing to pay. Or if someone takes out a hire-purchase agreement and doesn't pay the instalments, the finance company can sue him for breach of contract. The contract need not be in writing: an oral agreement to buy something from a shop or to do some work is just as much a contract as a document running to a dozen pages of legalese.

The great majority of actions in the civil courts are for money owed by one person to another – claims for unpaid debts, rent arrears or hire purchase payments; claims by suppliers of goods, workmen or professional people who have not been paid, or by the Inland Revenue for outstanding tax. Very few of these cases go to trial. In most of them there is nothing to argue about. The person sued usually owes the money but is in genuine financial difficulties, or simply trying to avoid payment. Receiving a claim form starting formal court proceedings, which shows him that his creditor is serious and is not willing to write him off as a bad debt, will often produce payment without further ado, if the money is there. For most money claims, unless the debtor can show some defence within the time allowed – for example, shoddy workmanship or faulty goods – the creditor gets a judgment in his favour without any sort of hearing.

Personal injury claims, although they account for a much smaller number of actions started in the civil courts, are more likely to go to trial, because they more often involve an argument about where the blame lies, and provide more scope for disagreement over the size of the claim. In the Queen's Bench Division of the High Court, which deals with the more serious tort cases and the larger money claims, the bulk of the cases which get as far as a trial are personal injury claims.

## Negligence

Anne Jones is unquestionably worse off than she was before the accident. She suffers from almost constant back pain, made worse if she sits for any length of time; her wrist is stiff and painful; she has headaches and can't enjoy life as she used to. It's impossible for her to continue doing her previous job, and she has had to take on less demanding, less well-paid work. She still suffers from headaches.

Yet Anne Jones is lucky. There is someone she can clearly point to as the author of her misfortune – John Smith, already branded as a careless driver by a criminal court. Getting compensation through the courts depends on pinning the blame on someone else. But some accidents are really nobody's fault. In one freak car crash the driver died of a heart attack seconds before his car collided with a motor-cycle. Because it wasn't the driver's fault, the motor-cyclist, who was seriously injured, got no compensation. Sometimes accident victims fail in their claims because they were entirely to blame for their own injuries. Anne Jones is fortunate not to have to prove that John Smith was negligent. The fact that he was convicted of careless driving has really established the point for her.

If John Smith had been acquitted by the jury, it would not have spoiled Anne's chances of claiming entirely, but it would have made it more difficult. It is quite possible for someone to be acquitted of a criminal charge and still be found negligent by a civil court. This is because the standard of proof is stricter in criminal cases. A jury or magistrates will only convict someone if they are sure beyond all reasonable doubt that he committed the crime, but in a civil case the judge only has to decide whose evidence is right 'on a balance of probabilities'. In other words, in Anne Jones's case against John Smith, which is more probable: that he was negligent or that he was not?

Proving negligence can be one of the biggest hurdles for accident victims. Sometimes there is no real evidence one way or the other. There may have been no witnesses to the accident. Cases like these are very much a legal lottery. In one case, a seven-year-old boy was struck by a car while riding his bicycle, and suffered brain damage. The High Court awarded him large damages. But the Court of Appeal set the award aside, ruling that no negligence had been proved.

The law can be very unfair. Suppose three men are crippled as the result of three different accidents. The first has an accident at work, the second is hit by a car, and the third damaged during surgery. Their relative chances of winning compensation through the courts are widely different. The work accident victim is best off. Employers have a number of special duties laid down by Parliament, for example, to fence dangerous machinery. If they fail in any of these duties, an injured employee is entitled to compensation without proving negligence. In many cases, a worker will be able to sue his employers for negligence as well, giving him two bites at the cherry. The road accident victim can only rely on negligence, and this is sometimes hard to prove. But in medical mishaps, proving fault is much more difficult. Many road accidents are caused by drivers who take obvious risks, drunk drivers, for example. With doctors, there are many more cases on the borderline between negligence and mere error of judgement. The difficulty of deciding on which side of the borderline a doctor's action falls is illustrated by the case of a handicapped baby, Stuart Whitehouse, born with severe brain damage. His mother said the doctor had pulled too long and hard on the forceps. She sued the doctor and the hospital and won large damages in the High Court. But the Court of Appeal reversed the decision. The doctor's use of the forceps did not amount to negligence, said the judges. It was simply an error of judgement, such as any competent doctor could have made. The House of Lords agreed. So the baby's parents got no compensation.

Victims of medical accidents face an additional hurdle. They have to prove not only that the doctor or health authority was negligent, but that the negligence caused their injury. In work or road accidents, the cause is usually obvious, but in medical cases it's often arguable that the patient's condition was caused by his illness or something else outside the doctor's control. Take the case of Martin Wilsher, a nearly blind nine-year-old whose case went to the House of Lords in 1988. Born prematurely, he was given too much oxygen in the special care baby unit. The High Court found the health authority negligent and awarded him damages. But the House of Lords said the original judge had misunderstood the evidence and the law. Blindness has been associated with a number of other conditions common in premature babies, and the evidence had not singled out the excess oxygen from other possible causes. Medical negligence claims have a far lower success rate than the 90 per cent for personal injury cases overall.

Despite the high success rate for most types of accidents, comparatively few accident victims make claims, for reasons discussed in Chapter I: lack of awareness of their rights, fear of the cost, not knowing how to go about it. High on the list of deterrents is fear of going to court – most people wrongly expect actually to have to appear in court to get compensation. The reality is that only one in a hundred personal injury claims started ever gets to court, and many of those that do are settled at the door of the court or during the trial, without the judge having to make a decision. Indeed, the vast majority of successful claims are settled even before a claim form has been issued. (A claim form is the document that starts a civil action: until 1999 it was known as a writ for cases in the High Court, or a summons, for the county court. Many lawyers, unwilling to break or incapable of breaking a lifetime's habit, continue to use the familiar and ancient terms writ and summons.)

## Starting the action

Anne Jones knows only one solicitor, who had dealt with her divorce a few years before. She thinks of going to see him, but fortunately speaks to a colleague first, who advises her to try to find a solicitor with particular experience in handling personal injury claims. This is good advice. Legal practice these days is becoming increasingly specialized, and it's possible that a small solicitors' firm that does a lot of criminal or family law work won't know a lot about fighting personal injury cases. As described in Chapter I, Anne Jones finds out from the Law Society the names of solicitors on their personal injury panel. She sees Mr Long, from a firm near her home.

He reassures her on two main concerns: first, he is willing to take on her case on a no-win, no-fee basis (known more formally as a conditional fee agreement, described in Chapter XI). Second, the fact that Smith was found guilty of careless driving, even though acquitted of dangerous driving, is very much in her favour. He tells her that there should be no difficulty in proving that he was negligent and therefore she should be able to recover compensation – known as damages – against him. It is because the case seems straightforward enough that Mr Long is willing to risk taking it under no-win, no-fee. If it had been more complex, for instance if it had been more difficult to prove Smith's negligence, the solicitor might have thought twice before taking on the case, with the risk that he might lose and get nothing for his work.

In Anne Jones's case, the only real question is, how much damages would she get? Her solicitor asks her the details of the accident and her injuries. She tells him that since the accident she has suffered from persistent headaches and bad back trouble. One wrist was broken and is still stiff. As a result of all this, she has found herself unable to go back to her old job as a graphic designer for a successful on-line IT magazine, and has been forced to go freelance, with a big cut in earnings. Mr Long also asks her in detail about the effect the injuries have had on her personal and family life; and questions her about her financial position.

Anne Jones leaves her solicitor's office an hour later. She has embarked on a long and difficult journey through the legal system.

The solicitor now takes over. John Smith was insured and her claim will in effect be against his insurance company. Although the legal proceedings will still be against Smith, in practice he fades out of the picture and the insurers take all the decisions. Most successful negligence claims are covered by insurance. Drivers have to insure against causing harm to other road users and employers must insure against injury to their employees. Most businesses carry public liability insurance, to cover claims by customers or anyone else injured in the course of their business activities. Many householders are covered against injury to tradesmen and visitors. Since the insurance company's money is at stake, it takes over complete control of the action as soon as it is notified of a claim.

The person claiming compensation may be put at an immediate disadvantage. The insurance company's solicitors are specialists, with considerable skill and experience in dealing with negligence cases. Tactical skills are arguably more important than knowing the law, and they only come with dealing with cases in volume. Unlike Anne Jones, many victims still land up with lawyers who aren't specialists, because they may not know lawyers who are. Anne Jones is lucky. Her solicitor, Mr Long, has had a good deal of experience in this field.

## Damages

Anne Jones's claim is for damages for personal injuries sustained in a car accident. Damages vary widely depending on the kind of civil claim. Damages for breach of contract, for instance, are calculated differently from damages for libel, or for personal injury. What lies at the heart of all claims for damages is compensation – the law tries to compensate a claimant for a wrong done to him. Sometimes it is easy to work out how much the damages should be: if a shopkeeper sells something for an agreed sum of £100 and he is not paid, he sues the buyer for £100, and that is what he will get if he wins. But sometimes it is much more difficult. How much should a negligent motorist have to pay for knocking down a pedestrian and breaking his leg or skull? And how much is a person's reputation worth if a newspaper falsely tells the world that he is a crook?

There is the direct financial loss on which a precise figure can be placed, and the more nebulous, less easy to quantify, compensation for pain and suffering, loss of future earnings, and other future losses. Anne Jones will be entitled, first, to money she has actually spent: medical and nursing bills, or damaged clothing, for instance, as well as lost earnings – most employers will carry a sick employee for a few weeks but can rarely keep him or her on full pay for months. These quantifiable amounts are called 'special damages'. Usually they are agreed between the two sides, as in Anne Jones's case.

The disputes usually concern the less precise items. Anne Jones is claiming for pain and suffering, both past and future. Her wrist was broken, her back injured and she gets headaches which may go on for some time. Her injuries could have been much more serious. She could have been disfigured or severely disabled, in which case she would have been entitled to very much larger sums of compensation. In some cases damages are given for 'loss of amenity' – the inability to take part in activities previously enjoyed, like sport, dancing or sex. It is obviously very difficult to put a precise figure on the value of particular injuries, but in practice lawyers get guidance from the awards given by judges in previous similar cases. These are collated and regularly updated in books on damages. So lawyers will know, for instance, that as a rough guide an amputated finger is worth around £6000 and the loss of an eye in the £25,000 to £30,000 range. These sums seem extremely low, and there has been persistent criticism of the mean level of damages awarded by English judges for pain, suffering, mental distress, grief, loss of amenities of life and other not easily quantifiable losses, and calls for levels to be raised substantially, if necessary by legislation. In 1999 the Law Commission, the government's legal think-tank, recommended that the amounts should be up to double the current level. In 2000, the Court of Appeal, at a special hearing, laid down new guidance for the amounts to be awarded in compensation for pain and suffering. Hopes that the court would follow the Law Commission's proposal to double damages were dashed. The appeal judges ruled that, for the most serious cases, such awards should be increased by up to a third; for less serious injuries, a smaller percentage uplift would apply. Anne Jones brought her case before the new guidance; in future the figures will be higher, but not dramatically so.

Anne Jones is also claiming for future loss of earnings. In her case she is asking for the difference between the salary she used to get in her old job and the lower income she earns as a freelance. For some people an accident can mean the permanent loss of promotion prospects, and for that, too, compensation is payable.

Those categories apply to damages for personal injuries. They are slightly different for other kinds of damages claims, but the way of assessing damages is similar: actual financial loss, plus compensation for more intangible results. A businessman suing for breach of contract, for instance, might claim lost future profits. In some cases it is enough just to put the claimant in the financial position he would have been in but for the wrong done to him. In many other categories, personal injuries being one, the law attempts the impossible task of putting a monetary value on something for which money is no real compensation.

## Civil justice radically reformed

In 1999, the laws and rules for settling civil disputes underwent a revolution. It wasn't just the procedures themselves that changed; what was also needed was a change in the philosophy and culture of litigation, and in the mind-set of the lawyers and the judges.

The old civil justice system suffered from three great weaknesses – it was expensive, it was lengthy and riddled with delays, and it was complex. Those three factors were interrelated. The process was pricey because the rules were so complex, which was also part of the reason for the delays. In addition, it was a system which was at the mercy of the lawyers, whose ability to exploit the rules – quite legally – often exacerbated the delays and cost. A further factor was that the procedure was aimed far more at fighting cases than at trying to settle them at an early stage of the dispute.

When in 1994 Lord Woolf, a law lord was first given the task of modernizing the system, his objective was to create one that was cheaper, quicker, simpler to use and available to more people; that would have as its aim the civilized resolution of legal disputes, not an all-out battle in the courts. Part of that aim required that the judges, who, until 1999, were little more than the final arbiters of the quarrel, became the controllers of the litigation – no longer would it be left to the lawyers to dawdle their way through a case. Efficiency, firm timetables, strict judges – all of them unknown concepts in civil justice – would become the norm. Even some of the centuries-old legal terminology was scrapped and replaced by more modern words: no more writs, only claim forms, no more plaintiffs, just claimants. All this, of course, at least in theory, is meant to be for the benefit of the ordinary person embroiled in the law, to turn what was a legal maze into a well sign-posted path.

## The early negotiations

Before even considering starting legal proceedings, Mr Long wants to explore the possibility of settling the case at an early stage. He is anxious to avoid the costs that start mounting up once formal proceedings get under way. Because it is unlikely that the insurance company will deny John Smith's liability, he hopes that he can get a deal on the amount of damages. It is a fact that the vast majority of accident claims are settled with the insurers within a few months.

Mr Long writes to John Smith's insurance company with a view to starting negotiations for a settlement. But before he can even begin discussions, he has to know the kind of sums that would be involved. To determine that, it is necessary for Anne Jones to undergo a medical examination by an expert. With the insurance company's agreement, the solicitor arranges for her to see Mr Collins, a consultant orthopaedic surgeon.

Mr Collins says in his report that Anne Jones had suffered a fracture of the lumbar vertebrae which was causing her continuing pain and discomfort. But he also mentions that she has had a history of recurrent attacks of back pain since childhood, which had required occasional physiotherapy and some absences from work – factors which will become important to her case. He concludes:

It is now ten months since this accident and it appears that this woman is now left with permanent stiffness of her dominant right wrist, which will cause her considerable difficulty doing all kinds of daily activities for the foreseeable future. Because of the persistent symptoms in her wrist and back, and her persistent headaches, it appears doubtful at the present time whether she is able to work as a computer graphic designer.

Her persistent back symptoms prevent her from sitting in one position for any length of time, and in particular it seems that she is unable to sit at, and work on, a computer screen for long periods. Her persistent headaches prevent her from concentrating and she has to lie down at times during the day. She still requires analgesic tablets.

In conclusion this woman has not fully recovered from her injuries, and it seems that she may well in fact never do so. It is unlikely that she will ever return to her previous occupation and may have to be content with less demanding jobs. Although some improvement may yet take place, it is unlikely that this will be significant.

For all practical purposes, therefore, her present situation can be taken as permanent.

Mr Long sends a copy of the medical report to the insurance company, hoping they'll agree with it and start talking about how much they're prepared to offer. But the insurers aren't happy. There's a lot of money at stake, and they arrange for Anne Jones to see their own consultant orthopaedic surgeon, Mr Greenfield. His report is very different and much more sceptical. He says, for instance, that although six months after the accident the hospital noted her to be fit for work and discharged her: '. . . it appears that she did not immediately return to full-time work.' He puts far greater emphasis on her previous back pains than did Mr Collins. Mr Greenfield concludes:

It was my general assessment with this patient that she was of a rather highly strung and nervous temperament, possessing a somewhat low pain threshold. In my opinion the stiffness in her wrist has persisted for this length of time because she has not made any concerted effort to use the wrist normally, nor has she seriously undergone any physiotherapy treatment which might have helped her condition.

In my opinion the injury to the back has been an exacerbation of the previous back weakness. When I questioned her closely on the severity of her back symptoms, she admitted to me that her symptoms now were not significantly different to her symptoms prior to the accident, and this is confirmed by the relative absence of physical findings on clinical examination today. Although there are signs of a fracture of the lumbar vertebrae, I am not satisfied that the back condition she complains of was brought about wholly by her accident. Mrs Jones finds herself in a somewhat unfortunate situation having to live on her own and support, unaided, a child, and it would seem to me that the strain of these responsibilities has been rather much for her and has adversely affected her ability to recover from what were, in fact, relatively short-term injuries.

Her persistent headaches are, in my opinion, not post-concussional and are more likely psychological in origin, precipitated by her unfortunate situation.

With regard to her ability to work, it is my assessment that there is no reason for her not being able to return to her previous occupation, or something similar, immediately. In my view, and apparently in the view of the doctors at the hospital who were looking after her, she was able physically to return to such work about six months after this accident.

If the two medical reports had agreed about her injuries and their continuing effect, the insurance company and Anne Jones's solicitor would almost certainly have reached agreement on a figure, after a period of bargaining. But the two experienced doctors disagree fundamentally. They are, in money terms, tens of thousands of pounds apart. Negotiations break down. The time has come for Mr Long to issue a claim form. The skirmishes have ended. Battle has officially commenced. The complex game that is civil litigation is under way.

## Before the trial

For Anne Jones, the first question that arises is: which court will hear her claim? Personal injury cases can take place either in the High Court or the county courts. If the claim is for less than £15,000 there is a special 'fast-track' procedure, with its own rules, aimed, as the name suggests, at a speedy resolution. Under fast-track, even before any formal claim form is issued, claimants are expected to follow a 'pre-action protocol' (so much for simple language), which lays down all the steps that need to be taken, including providing all the particulars of the injury and other information. The idea is to give the other side – the defendant, in effect usually his insurance company – a detailed idea of what the claim is all about, in the hope that negotiations can soon begin to settle the claim, without the need for formal proceedings.

Anne Jones's claim is clearly worth far more than £15,000, so she isn't in the fast-track. Her path is the 'multi-track'. The parties are not required to use the pre-action protocol, but are urged to follow it as far as they can and to exchange as much information as possible, so that any possible early settlement can be explored. In effect, Anne Jones's lawyers and the insurance company's have done this, by exchanging the crucial medical reports and trying to find some area of compromise.

The fact that Anne Jones's claim is 'multi-track' doesn't automatically define what court her claim will go to. Usually, if it's worth more than £50,000, it will be in the High Court, less than that in the county court. Anne Jones's lawyers carefully do the sums. They cannot see how, on their own expert's opinion of her injuries and how they will affect her future, her claim can possibly be less than £50,000. So it's a clearly a case for the High Court.

Anne Jones's claim form gives particulars of the accident, the negligence she alleges against John Smith, and the injuries she suffered. Mr Collins's report is attached, and a list of the special damages she's claiming, the amounts that can be quantified, like medical bills.

The insurer's lawyers, on the basis of their medical expert's opinion, have no alternative but to defend what they regard as a grossly inflated claim. There follows a highly procedural exchange of information, key documents and medical reports. The aim, under the Woolf reforms, is for each side to know exactly what the other side's case is – it's a 'cards on the table' approach, in contrast to the more 'cards close to the chest' that the law used to allow. Before they get to court, the contestants should know everything that's crucial about each other's case. Last minute surprises are not on the agenda.

During this whole pre-trial skirmishing, the judge allocated to the case will be keeping a close watch to see whether more attempts can be made to settle the dispute without going to court. The Woolf reforms place at centre stage the concept of 'alternative dispute resolution', the most common example of which is the process of mediation. A trained mediator sits at a table with the warring parties (and their lawyers) and attempts to help them identify and narrow down their points of difference, and if possible reach some form of compromise. The mediator does not decide anything, nor lay down solutions; he does not act as a judge. He is a facilitator, go-between and neutral aid to negotiation, who can sometimes help break a deadlock.

The judge allocated to Anne Jones's case thinks there is a chance that the two sides, though apparently far apart, might be helped by mediation. He strongly suggests that they try it. They do, but it's fruitless. Also at the suggestion of the judge, the two orthopaedic experts meet to discuss Anne Jones's medical condition and prognosis, but they continue to disagree fundamentally.

Both sets of lawyers know how much legal costs can escalate once the trial approaches, and how uncertain the trial result can be. They have sincerely tried to settle the case; but they are too far apart. A full-scale court battle looks inevitable. But there is still one tactic left to the defendant – a device known as a payment into court (now officially called a Part 36 payment). It can be used in all kinds of civil cases when the amount is in dispute, not just in personal injuries claims.

## Payment into court ( Part 36 payment)

The point of a payment into court is to put pressure on a claimant to accept an offer of settlement from the defendant, and so avoid having to go to trial. It's a sum of money literally deposited with the court by the defendant – in effect John Smith's insurance company – in final settlement of the claimant's – Anne Jones's – claim. She must now decide either to take the money or to reject it and pursue the case to trial.

But there is a catch: if she refuses the offer and at the end of the trial the judge awards her the same amount or less than the payment in, she will probably have to pay not only her own costs, but also those of her opponent, from the date the payment was made. And the legal costs can be huge.

In a case in 1992 (before the new rules), the *Coronation Street* actor Bill Roache sued the *Sun* for libel for describing him as 'boring' and disliked by the rest of the cast. He won, and the jury awarded him £50,000. Coincidentally the *Sun* had previously made a payment into court of exactly that sum: £50,000 (the jury didn't know this). But, because they hadn't awarded him more, Roache had to pay a large slice of the *Sun*'s legal costs. Although he'd won the case and received £50,000, he found himself tens of thousands of pounds out of pocket. Had the jury awarded him £50,001, the *Sun* would have had to pay his costs, instead of the other way around.

Cases like Roache's, where a difference of a few pounds awarded by judge or jury can in real terms mean many thousands of pounds one way or the other, demonstrate the iniquities of the law. Now, a judge has some discretion in awarding legal costs, if he thinks the rule would operate unjustly. In a future case like Roache's the judge might be able to say, for instance, that Roache wouldn't have to pay all the *Sun*'s costs, only a part of them.

It is now also possible (which it wasn't before) for the claimant – the Anne Jones figure – to make a formal offer of settlement. It works like a Part 36 payment in reverse – if the judge awards the claimant more than the settlement offer, the defendant has to pay much of the legal costs, as punishment for having dragged the proceedings out when it could have settled for a lower amount.

Back to Anne Jones's case. The insurance company is working out how much to offer in a Part 36 payment. It has to be calculated carefully to make it tempting enough for Anne Jones to take it. The insurance company's solicitor and their claims manager hold a conference with their barrister, Mr Green. The defence stick by the conclusion of Mr Greenfield's report that Anne Jones's injuries are not as severe as she has painted them, that they are not long-lasting, that they're partly due to a previously existing condition and that she could go back to her old kind of job if she wanted to. They assess the general damages she might get at a maximum of £15,000 and add the special damages (medical bills and other money already spent, and past loss of earnings), which are at the time around £7000. Then they add a little to make the offer slightly more tempting, and also add a further amount for interest. Eventually the lawyers reach a figure of £28,000 to be paid into court.

The pressure is now on Anne Jones to respond. It is a crucial decision. Should she go on in the hope that she can get more, but take the risk that she might land up with very little once the costs have been taken care of? She needs counsel's advice on whether or not to accept. She goes with her solicitor to the Middle Temple chambers of Mr Grey, the barrister who has been briefed in her case.

Mr Grey has read the medical reports and notices the discrepancies between them. He needs to test the strengths and weaknesses of Anne Jones's case before reaching a conclusion. For more than an hour he questions her about every detail of her medical condition. At the end of it he is broadly satisfied that Anne Jones is being truthful, and that Mr Greenfield's report is not altogether reliable. Mr Grey believes that she will get about £35,000 for past and future pain and suffering (the headaches, back and wrist pains) and loss of amenities (no sport, painful sex). He also takes the view, contrary to that of Mr Greenfield and the insurance company, that she will not be able to take on a job that pays as much as she used to earn. He thinks that for at least five years she will lose £7000 a year in income. The five years is an arbitrary time period. It is quite low because Mr Grey thinks that she may recover from the effects of her injuries to some extent, or that her financial circumstances might change. He also adds £8000 for paying someone to do the housekeeping for a few years – tasks that her injuries prevent her from doing. With the special damages and interest (£7000), the total comes to £85,000 – more than three times the sum paid into court by the insurance company.

Mr Grey warns her that she will still be taking a bit of a gamble by rejecting the payment in, but:

MR GREY: In those circumstances the risk that you face, if you don't accept the money that's now in court, in my view, is very slight. Had they paid a sum in of, say, £60,000 or something of that order, I'm bound to say that my advice would be very much less confident.

*ANNE JONES*: I'm not really prepared to accept that amount of money. I think it is too little and it is not just that. I feel that having got this far, I want to take it all the way.

She, in her turn, advised by her lawyers, decides to make a Part 36 offer to settle. They're pretty sure she won't get less than £55,000 if it gets to court. She's in effect saying to Smith's insurance company: 'Give me that sum now, the case is finished, and you're not in danger of paying my huge legal bill if the judge eventually gives me more.' The insurance company isn't interested.

Anne Jones is gambling with a lot of money. The whole payment into court process creates risk and puts the individual claimant under stress. In theory the procedure exists to discourage frivolous or speculative actions. The idea is that no one will wish to continue unless he believes he has a genuine case. It is also meant to stop dragging matters out unnecessarily.

The pressure to settle does not, however, fall evenly on the two sides. Very often, especially in actions for personal injuries arising out of accidents, it is a fight between David (albeit helped by a lawyer) and Goliath, the individual versus the big insurance company. It is equally uneven in many cases where, for instance, big stores or companies sue customers for money allegedly owing – the individual may believe he does not owe the money, or that the goods are defective, but he is often overwhelmed by the prospect of taking on the big battalions.

The individual claimant wants to get the whole case over with as soon as possible – not only so that he can get his hands on the money quickly, but also because of the constant stress and emotional tension that involvement in a legal action usually brings. A company feels no such pressures and it is often in its interests in borderline cases to string out the proceedings and wear down the other side. The personal strain is enormous. For an insurance company a legal claim is a matter of business; for the individual it is something the result of which can affect his whole life. While the case is going on, it can dominate it. Often, of course, the legal proceedings follow another nasty experience – an accident. Many litigants succumb to the strain and give up the legal battle by withdrawing or settling on inadequate terms. Anne Jones, however, perseveres. Eventually, two years after the accident, the case is listed for trial in the High Court.

## The day of the trial

A little after ten o'clock in the morning Anne Jones and her solicitor arrive at court. They are early so that they can have a few final words with her barrister, Mr Grey, and her doctor, Mr Collins, who will be a witness about her medical condition. There is also a good chance that they will be offered more money, even at this late stage. Perhaps as many as a third of cases that reach court are settled literally at the doors. High Court judge Mr Justice Wright explains:

This is really the time when everybody begins to face up to the realities. The plaintiff, who may up to that point have been making extravagant claims for the size of his claim or the amount of money that he's lost, now realizes that he has to go into the witness box, take the oath and persuade a judge of the validity of what he is saying. And it's usually at this stage that possibly an element of cold feet begins to creep into the negotiations.

Equally the defendant and his advisers have to face up to the fact that their evidence may not be as strong as they hope, and they may not be able to produce so powerful a defence. The parties are there, seeing each other face to face; they are able to take immediate instructions from their clients, from their witnesses, from their experts, and make a final assessment of the strengths or weaknesses of their case.

To that can be added the fact that by this time they know who the judge is going to be, and whether he has a reputation for being stingy or generous.

A few yards away from Anne Jones and her team, in the corridor outside the courtroom where the trial is to take place, the opposing side is talking in low whispers. Mr Simms, the insurance company's solicitor, tells Mr Green, their barrister, that they are willing to raise the offer to £40,000 – £12,000 more than the amount they paid into court.

In a scene duplicated thousands of times every year outside

hundreds of courtrooms, in the county courts as well as the High Court, the defendant's barrister approaches the claimant's to tell him of the last-minute offer aimed at avoiding a full-blown trial. Mr Green tells Mr Grey that his clients will offer £40,000 but no more. Mr Grey is certain that Anne Jones will not be interested in that figure, but he is duty bound to convey the new offer to her. Anne Jones wants to reject it and her solicitor and barrister agree. The barristers meet again and Mr Grey informs his opponent of Anne Jones's rejection. The insurance company is not prepared to go any higher, so the trial will have to go ahead.

There is no jury. The judge alone will decide. In Anne Jones's case his job will be limited to only one decision – how much to award her. Because the insurance company has admitted that John Smith's driving was at fault, the judge will not have to rule on who was to blame, something which is very often in dispute. He will not even have to make up his mind on whether Anne Jones was partly to blame – guilty of contributory negligence. If all these issues were still in dispute it would have been a much longer trial. For the claimant, Anne Jones, witnesses would have been called to testify that John Smith was driving carelessly; that he was going far too fast in the circumstances, so that he wasn't able to avoid hitting her. It would have been, to a large extent, a rehash of the evidence called at Smith's Crown Court trial.

The defence would have found it difficult to claim that Smith was totally faultless, but it might have argued that Anne Jones played her part in the accident by stepping off the kerb when it was not safe to do so. It would have been put to her in cross-examination that she had not looked properly to see whether there was anything coming. It is possible that, after hearing all the witnesses, the judge might have found Anne Jones guilty of some contributory negligence. This is expressed in percentage terms, so Anne Jones might have been, say, 25 per cent to blame. This would not have lost her the case altogether, but it would have reduced her damages by that percentage.

But perhaps the most important effect of fighting not only about damages but also about liability is that it adds a new dimension to the decision about whether to accept a payment into court. If there was a chance of losing the case, or having her damages reduced because of her own contributory negligence, she would obviously have been far more disposed to accept the offer. The result of a court case is never certain and many lawyers advise their clients to accept the bird in the hand. All this is academic in Anne Jones's case. The insurance company were faced with a verdict of guilty of careless driving against John Smith. That hardly augured well for a successful defence of the civil claim, with its easier burden of proof. The insurance company therefore decided to throw in the towel on liability and fight on 'quantum' – how much.

One other important issue has been decided in the days leading up to the trial. Under the 1999 reforms, judges have the power to order that, instead of both sides being allowed to call their own expert witnesses (whether medical or in any other field) to give evidence on their behalf, there should be only one, impartial, expert providing a report to the judge. The reason for that reform was that, too often, especially in relatively simple cases, it was a waste of time and money to have two highly-paid experts giving evidence in court; a single expert, appointed by the court, could examine the victim and inform the judge of his conclusions, thus shortening and simplifying trials. In Anne Jones's case the lawyers on both sides are against a single court expert. They tell the judge that the doctors are very far apart in their views, not just in their assessment of Anne Jones's future, but of her truthfulness. This is something a judge should decide. The judge agrees. He does not order a court expert and tells the two sides that they can each call their own expert.

# The trial

The English civil trial, like its criminal counterpart, is conducted on adversarial lines. There are two contestants, each having free rein through their lawyers to run the case as they see fit, and to call or not call what witnesses they want. The judge is the sole arbiter both of fact and of law. He seldom intervenes, even if he feels that one or other side has not called a key witness. As in criminal trials, many cases are won and lost on tactics and advocacy rather than on where the truth lies.

The trial begins with the claimant's counsel, Mr Grey, outlining Anne Jones's case. The judge has previously read through the various documents, including the medical reports, and has some idea of what the trial is about. But he does not know that there has been a Part 36 payment into court, and even if he suspects there has been one (it is a relatively common practice) he does not know how much it is. Anne Jones's barrister summarizes the circumstances of the accident, and explains that the crux of the case is the disagreement between the two doctors. Her own medical expert, Mr Collins, says that she may never recover fully from the injuries she received to her wrist and back, and from her headaches. As a result she is unable to go back to her old full-time job as a computer graphic designer and has had to work as a freelance from home, part-time, doing far less challenging work for less money. He admits that the defence medical expert, Mr Greenfield, believes that Anne Jones's symptoms are exaggerated, that her problems are mainly psychological and that she could return to something similar to her old work if she wanted to; but, says Mr Grey, Anne Jones rejects those allegations.

After his opening speech the first witness is called. Anne Jones herself takes the oath and embarks on what is for her a vital hour. The impression she makes on the judge is crucial. If he thinks she is telling the truth about the effect of her injuries, then the amount of damages is likely to be close to what she is hoping for. But if he believes she is exaggerating, it will affect not only the amount of damages she gets but also her costs.

How does a judge know if a witness is telling the truth? An experienced judge explains:

One has to remember that judges are not infallible. We haven't got a crystal ball into which we can gaze and get the answers to whether or not the witness is truthful. And I would be the first to admit I may have been led up the garden on various occasions. But having made these qualifications, I think over the years – and remember one has twenty years at the Bar probably before going on the bench – one builds up a sort of inbred sense of whether the witness is telling the truth, exaggerating, or simply telling a pack of lies. And that is quite apart from the testing of the witness's evidence against the evidence of other witnesses. And witnesses of course can be mistaken. It's more often the case that they're mistaken, or their recollection is faulty, than that they're deliberately lying. The deliberate really good liar is probably pretty difficult to detect.

Anne Jones's counsel is concerned about the suggestion in Mr Greenfield's report that she has not tried very hard to overcome her injuries, and did not go back to work as soon as she could have. He asks her about her first day back at work at her old company, six months after the accident:

*ANNE JONES*: Well, I went to the department I used to work in, and by lunchtime I was feeling very bad indeed. I suddenly realized that I couldn't actually sit still at the computer screen for the length of time that was needed. And the next morning if anything it was worse. It was very painful when I woke up. And I'm afraid that I had to leave at lunchtime. I couldn't even see the job through until the end of the day.

She sums up her symptoms as they are, two years after the accident:

The back is as bad as it was two weeks after the accident. I haven't noticed any difference, any improvement at all in the pain. My headaches are again just as bad, I get them two or three times a week since the accident. My left and right wrists are a lot better obviously. My left wrist is still a bit stiff. The right wrist, I just can't seem to carry heavy things in it, and I do have a difficulty key-stroking. There are just certain movements that I find rather difficult to do with my right wrist – it's still very stiff.

The judge intervenes, and asks her to grip his arm, to test how hard she can grip.

Anne Jones then gives evidence about other consequences of her injuries. She can no longer play badminton or ski, both of which she used to do enthusiastically; and she finds it uncomfortable to have sex, which resulted in problems with her boyfriend and the end of their relationship. She has also become frightened to cross roads, and has flashbacks of the accident.

At the end of Anne Jones's evidence, it is the turn of Mr Green, the defence barrister, to cross-examine. His task is to dent the good impression she seems to have made. He asks her detailed questions about how she uses her wrist, trying to show that she could key-stroke more easily than she admits. He tries to emphasize inconsistencies between what she told Mr Greenfield, according to his report, and what she said in court. He probes an apparent discrepancy about her back. Mr Greenfield's report said that she told him that the back pain was not very different from what it had been before the accident. If that is so, it suggests that the accident was not, or only marginally, to blame.

*ANNE JONES*: No, that really was a misunderstanding, because what I said to him was that the area of the pain was not any different. In other words, I was getting the pain in the same area that I used to get the pain when I was a child. And the pain was a similar sort of pain. But this is ten times worse than anything I'd had as a child.

At the end of his cross-examination of Anne Jones, the defence barrister, Mr Green, is reasonably satisfied that he has sown some doubts about her backache, which she has said is her main problem.

The only other witness for the claimant is Mr Collins, Anne Jones's consultant orthopaedic surgeon. He repeats more or less what he said in his report. The case has clearly come down to a straight question of Anne Jones's truthfulness. At the end of Mr Collins's evidence, the claimant's case is closed.

Mr Green, the barrister for the insurance company, does not need to make an opening speech: the issue is clear enough. In a more complicated case he might have given the judge a brief outline of the main points, but these speeches by counsel in a civil case are not as important as they are in criminal trials, where there is an untrained jury who have to have the case explained to them in simple terms.

The only witness for the defence is Mr Greenfield. The most crucial point for the defence is his opinion of Anne Jones's back injury, which she has said was the main reason she couldn't go back to her old job. Mr Greenfield repeats that he had understood from her that the back pain was much the same as she had suffered from before the accident. He accepts that the accident might have exacerbated it, but only to a mild degree. It is vital for Anne Jones's case that the judge should not believe Mr Greenfield's version. Her counsel, Mr Grey, starts his cross-examination by trying to establish that the meeting between him and Anne Jones was tense and that the two did not get on very well. Mr Greenfield denies this. He concedes, however, that he might have been mistaken in saying that Anne Jones had not tried to go back to work as soon as she could. This misunderstanding has an effect on the whole of the cross-examination. Mr Greenfield's admission that he might have misinterpreted what she said on this point puts a question mark against the rest of his evidence.

The next important area for the claimant's barrister to probe concerns Anne Jones's back injury. Mr Greenfield has recorded in his report that the back was no worse than before the accident. Mr Grey questions Mr Greenfield.

*MR GREY*: In her evidence to the court, she said she certainly wasn't telling you that it was the same as the pre-accident state had been. And yet that was your impression, according to your report.

*MR GREENFIELD*: That was what my impression was at the time from what she told me.

*MR GREY*: Nonetheless, you knew that she was continuing to wear a corset, as necessary.

*MR GREENFIELD*: Yes.

*MR GREY*: Which would be inconsistent with the pre-accident condition that you would have expected her back to be in.

*MR GREENFIELD*: I think that certainly I would accept that she had suffered a little more back pain than she had previously. I'm prepared to accept that.

This will prove an important admission from Mr Greenfield. He is the only witness for the defence. The next stage is for both counsel to make their closing speeches, which are short – the trial has lasted only a few hours and the judge, unlike a jury, needs no spoonfeeding about the crucial issues.

The defendant's counsel is first to speak. He tries to play down Mr Greenfield's apparent back-tracking. He suggests also that Anne Jones's symptoms may in part be caused by worry about the litigation and will therefore disappear when the case ends.

It is also in the closing speeches that both sides outline what level of damages they think are appropriate under each heading. On future loss of earnings, the difference in earnings between Anne Jones's former job and her present work, Mr Green argues that no award at all should be made, on the strength of Mr Greenfield's opinion that nothing is stopping her from going back to her old job or something similar. He also says that no award should be made for housekeeping help, because she doesn't really need it. Mr Green suggests a figure of between £10,000 and £15,000 for pain and suffering. Special damages, the sum awarded for medical and other expenditure arising from the accident, are agreed at £8,500 (they have risen since the payment into court).

In his speech, Mr Grey, Anne Jones's barrister, asks the judge to accept her evidence and reject Mr Greenfield's findings. He claims £7000 a year for loss of future earnings, which he argues could go on for many years, as could her need for future housekeeping help, the cost of which he estimates at about £2000 a year. Pain and suffering, and loss of amenity, he suggests, should be compensated for by a payment of between £30,000 and £40,000.

Both sides have now had their say. It is up to the judge to decide. Unlike juries or magistrates in a criminal case, judges in civil cases give the reasons for their decisions. Often, the judge needs a few days, or sometimes weeks, to consider his decision and map out his reasoning. But Anne Jones's case was short and uncomplicated. He is able to give his decision immediately.

The judge starts off by briefly summarizing the facts of the case. He then gives his views on the contentious areas. First he deals with the suggestion that Anne Jones hadn't tried hard enough to go back to her old job.

*JUDGE*: I am quite satisfied that she made the effort to get back to work, that she simply couldn't do it; and that the hospital's conclusion that she was then fit for work is something to which I ought not to have any real regard.

On the headaches, which Mr Greenfield had suggested were largely psychological:

*JUDGE*: To say that it's psychological and arises from an accumulation of troubles, of divorce, being left with a young child, the litigation and so on, is only I think half the story, if it is half the story. The real causative factor of the headaches, it seems to me, was and still is the head injury.

Then he comes to the crucial question of Anne Jones's back:

*JUDGE*: I think whatever one may say about the back in the past, we always come back to the position that it wasn't troubling her just before the accident, it has troubled her since, it is troubling her now, and I am bound really to accept the evidence of Mr Collins, who says that there will be, in his view, a great possibility of trouble in the future.

The judge now comes to the important part of the decision: how much? For future loss of earnings, he awards £25,000. For house-keeping he gives £3000, because he doesn't believe Anne Jones will need help for long. For general damages, he settles on a figure of £30,000. And he awards the agreed special damages. The total comes to £66,500.

Anne Jones has done well. The damages she has been awarded are well above the final offer at the doors of the court, and more than twice the Part 36 payment into court, and more than the £55,000 she offered to settle at. This means that the judge orders the defendants, the insurance company, to pay her legal costs.

It is not quite finished for Anne Jones. There is still the possibility that the insurance company will appeal. There seems to be no point of law which they can contest – the case raises no legal issues. The only possible appeal is against the amount of damages. The Court of Appeal will usually interfere with an award of damages only if it is totally unreasonable, or made on the wrong legal basis. The insurance company may think that the amount Anne Jones got is too high, but it is clearly not absurdly high. They decide the chances of a successful appeal are very slim, and decide to leave matters alone.

It's often said that only people who've been involved in it can realize the uncertainty, the emotional energy and the anxiety that go into litigation. A speedier and simpler legal procedure may help, but can never fully take away the stress of fighting a legal battle.

Anne Jones's two-year legal ordeal is finally over. She pursued her case to the bitter end. But many like her have fallen along the way, because they didn't know their rights, or they couldn't afford the cost of litigation and couldn't find a lawyer to take it on no-win, no-fee, or because they lacked the determination or the stamina to carry on, and accepted inadequate offers of settlement just to relieve the pressure on them (though also, to be fair, some receive very good settlements). And finally there are those who overcome all the hurdles and have their trial – and lose.

## The Future

It may take years before we can assess whether the civil justice revolution has been a success in providing cheaper, quicker and less complex justice to more people, and in diverting the system away from its traditional confrontational stance and towards less heated mediation. The intentions of Lord Woolf's reforms are certainly to be praised; how far they are fulfilled in practice is another question. Early indications are that they are broadly successful and that fewer cases are coming to court.

There are still, though, commentators who believe that even the Woolf reforms are merely tinkering with a system that is fundamentally flawed. Compensation, they argue, should be removed from the legal system altogether, at least for some types of injury.

Lord Denning, in *What Next in the Law* (Butterworths, 1982), had this to say:

Our law as to personal injuries is entirely out of date. It evolved during the time when all civil actions were tried by juries and all damages were assessed by juries. It was formed in relation to horse transport and rail transport. It is quite inapplicable to transport by motor vehicles. These bring death and disablement on all sides. Many of those injured are unable to prove that the driver was negligent. It is imperative, as a matter of justice, that there should be introduced a system for compensation to victims even though they cannot prove negligence: no-fault liability as it is called.

He was supporting a recommendation of a 1978 Royal Commission under Lord Pearson which had proposed lifting most traffic accident victims out of the legal process altogether. No longer would compensation depend on pinning the blame on someone else. The new 'no-fault' system would remove the element of chance which can give thousands of pounds to one road accident victim, while another, with equally severe injuries, gets nothing – simply because the first happened to be knocked down in front of reliable witnesses with good memories, while the second was hit on a lonely stretch of road. The no-fault compensation scheme proposed would be administered by the state and funded by a small levy on petrol, thus in effect making motorists pay for the accidents and injuries motorists caused.

Ten years later, in 1988, another review of civil justice called on the Lord Chancellor to consider, in consultation with the insurance industry, the feasibility of a no-fault scheme restricted to less serious road accidents. Nothing has happened to either proposal, but there is still a strong body of expert opinion which believes that even a Woolf-reformed civil litigation system is wasteful of time and money, and, above all, unfair as between different accident victims.

In one area, no-fault compensation is still very much under discussion. The medical profession have been pressing the government from time to time to consider no-fault compensation for medical accidents. As recently as 1999, the House of Commons health select committee gave its support to no-fault compensation schemes for the National Health Service. Patients would no longer have to prove that someone was negligently to blame – only that there was a link between their treatment and their injury.

# CHAPTER VIII

# Divorce

Tens of thousands of accident victims start legal proceedings every year. Chapter VII charted the progress of just one of them, Anne Jones, through the legal system. But for many more people – around 300,000 a year – the accident which embroils them in the legal process is the breakdown of their marriage. This chapter follows Mary James, one of the 300,000, through the divorce machine.

Mary James is 31. She and her husband, Bill, have been married for ten years, and have two children – David, nine, and Paul, eight. Just over two years ago, Bill started going out with Jane, a girl at his office, and two months later he left Mary and moved in with Jane. Mary was devastated, but she kept hoping Bill would come to his senses and come back to her. He went on paying the mortgage and the household bills, very much as before. But gradually she has come to accept the fact that her marriage is over, and recently she has started seeing another man regularly, though she has no immediate intention of remarrying.

Now Bill is talking about selling the house, which he and Mary own jointly, and using his share to buy a new flat for himself and Jane. Mary is worried about her position, and decides to see a solicitor to find out what her rights are and to see about getting a divorce.

Divorce is part of the civil law. The process for sorting out disputes between divorcing spouses has a lot in common with an action for breach of contract or negligence. Usually each side is represented by a separate lawyer. Each puts forward his or her own side of the case. Most disputes are resolved by negotiation between lawyers, but if the case goes to court the judge decides the result, mainly on the evidence that the two sides put before the court.

But divorce sits uneasily as part of the judicial process. Decisions are based much more on welfare principles – such as the needs of the parties and the best interests of the children – and less on strict legal rights. Over the years many commentators have called for divorce to be removed from the ordinary courts and dealt with in special family courts, with more of a social welfare and less of a judicial emphasis, with husband and wife helped to reach their own agreements and the whole process conducted along more 'inquisitorial' – fact-finding – lines, rather than the present 'adversarial' approach, which tends to foster conflict. As Stephen Cretney, Fellow of All Souls College, Oxford, has put it: 'It may be argued that a system of accusatorial court hearings, almost inevitably institutionalizing the parties' hostility towards one another, is not well suited to the satisfactory resolution of family problems.' The need to accuse the other party of a matrimonial fault to obtain a quick divorce also raises the temperature. The Law Commission, the official law reform body, recognized this and in 1990 recommended a move to no-fault divorce. This was eventually accepted by the last Conservative government, and resulted in the Family Law Act 1996. However, the bill which became the Act provoked great controversy during its parliamentary passage, and was much amended. The result was a mishmash which many thought unworkable, and the Labour government which came to power in 1997 indefinitely shelved the part of the Act which would bring in no-fault divorce. However, other parts of the Act have been brought into force, including provisions aimed at encouraging those financially eligible for state funding to try to resolve their disputes through less expensive mediation rather than through the courts.

## Getting a divorce

At present all divorces start in the county court. Not every county court hears divorces, but some courts are designated divorce county courts and deal with divorces along with their other business. In London, the Principal Registry is the equivalent of a divorce county court.

Getting a divorce is now much simpler than it used to be. You no longer have to go to court and answer embarrassing questions about the reasons your marriage broke down. The whole process is just a matter of getting the paperwork right. Now that getting the divorce decree is largely a rubber-stamping exercise not much more difficult than filling in a tax return, the court battles revolve around what happens after the divorce: who will the children live with, and how often should the other parent see them? How is the property divided? How much maintenance, if any, should be paid?

The process starts with a petition for divorce which is filed with the court. A husband and wife cannot jointly petition for a divorce; one or the other must start the ball rolling. No one can petition for divorce within the first year of marriage.

Mary has a part-time job in an estate agents' office which brings in £175 a week. Bill gives her £200 a month for each child, so her income is too high to qualify for advice and help with preparing her petition from a Community Legal Service solicitor (*see* Chapter IX). She decides to handle the divorce herself and involve solicitors only in working out the long-term financial arrangements. In the Jameses' case, since Mary is asking for the divorce, she is known as the 'petitioner'. Bill is called the 'respondent'. About 70 per cent of divorces are started by wives, but exactly the same rules apply if the husband is petitioning for divorce.

Although official policy is firmly in favour of allowing dead marriages to be decently buried, divorce is still not available on demand. Grounds still have to be proved. Since 1971, the law says the only ground is that the marriage has 'irretrievably broken down'. The evidence of the breakdown is provided by proving one of five 'facts' (which, confusingly, many lawyers still refer to as 'grounds').

Mary's solicitor tells her that her petition will have to be based on one of the following:

*Fact A*: that her husband has committed adultery and she finds it intolerable to live with him.

*Fact B*: that her husband has behaved in such a way that she cannot reasonably be expected to live with him.

*Fact C*: that her husband has deserted her for a period of at least two
years.

*Fact D*: that she and her husband have lived apart for at least two
years, and he consents to the divorce.

*Fact E*: that she and her husband have lived apart for at least five years
(in this case, his consent is not necessary).

Theoretically, the concept of the 'guilty' party and the 'innocent'
party has gone from divorce. When divorce by consent was introduced, there were great hopes that it would lead to more civilized
divorces, but the hopes were unfounded. Adultery and 'unreasonable
behaviour' are still the most popular reasons for divorce – accounting
for 70 per cent of divorces – with divorce by consent trailing in third
place. It is no coincidence that the two most used facts are the only
ones which allow a quick divorce; the others all mean a wait of at least
two years. The vast majority of unreasonable behaviour petitions are
brought by wives, presumably wanting a quick divorce so that their
financial claims can be sorted out without delay.

There was a growing consensus during the 1980s that the existence
of the unreasonable behaviour fact was partly to blame for the knock-
down, drag-out battles over money, property and children which
some divorces became – often at great expense to the public purse,
since many were conducted with the help of legal aid. Airing the dirty
laundry of a rocky relationship – particularly when incidents in which
both sides may have been at fault are given a one-sided slant – is
hardly likely to put the spouse on the receiving end into a reasonable
frame of mind. These days, however, solicitors – particularly members
of the Solicitors' Family Law Association – pride themselves on adopting a conciliatory rather than an adversarial approach. Often the
lawyers for each side will agree in advance what the behaviour allegations should be, and draft them as inoffensively as possible.

In its 1990 proposals for divorce reform the Law Commission
recommended that the single ground for divorce should remain
irretrievable breakdown, but that the divorce should be granted on
demand, though only after a transition period of twelve months.
Either party, or both, would file a written statement that the marriage

had broken down. At the end of the transition period, either could apply for the divorce decree. In the meantime, there would be a period for reflection and for sorting out arrangements for children and property. Gwynn Davis and Mervyn Murch in their book *Grounds for Divorce* (Oxford University Press, 1988) found that the present system tended to rush couples into divorce without giving them time for second thoughts. The part of the Family Law Act which has now been shelved broadly adopted this approach, but in a more cumbersome form which would have meant a considerably longer wait for a divorce for most people than at present.

Mary decides to base her petition on two years' separation with Bill's consent. She has already discussed the question of divorce with Bill, and he says he won't object. A 'statement of arrangements' for the children will be sent to the court with the petition and the Jameses' marriage certificate. This gives the court details of the children's accommodation, schooling, financial support and arrangements for them to see their father.

The court sends Bill a copy of the divorce papers, which he acknowledges, confirming that he consents. Even where a divorce is not based on consent, in most cases the respondent will not raise any objections to the divorce. Many respondents whose first reaction is to 'defend' the divorce, to deny that the marriage has broken down or to object to the allegations made against them, are advised against it by their solicitors. Defending a divorce is usually a fruitless and expensive exercise, because most judges take the view that a marriage has irretrievably broken down if one party is determined to end it, irrespective of the feelings of the other partner in the marriage. Well over 99 per cent of divorces are undefended, like the Jameses'.

The court sends Mary a copy of Bill's acknowledgement. This is her cue to move on to the next stage, completing an affidavit, a sworn document confirming that the contents of the petition are true and that there are grounds for the divorce. Now that petitioners no longer have to appear in court, this takes the place of the oral evidence which used to be required.

The district judge will look at the papers and see that everything is in order and the case for the divorce has been made out, and will review the arrangements for the children. He will consider whether any court order needs to be made for the children – for instance, a residence order stating which parent they will live with. In most cases no order is needed. If there are doubts or concerns about the children or a clear dispute between the parents, further evidence will be called for.

If the district judge is satisfied with the petition he will certify that the divorce should be granted. The date is fixed for the judge to pronounce the divorce decree in open court. A list of names of couples to be divorced is read out and the judge simply states that each of them is granted a 'decree nisi'. There is no need for any of the couples to attend court. The decree nisi is only a provisional decree. The marriage is not finally ended until the decree is made absolute, usually six weeks later. Only after decree absolute has been pronounced are the parties free to marry again.

Mary's proposals for the children were set out in the 'statement of arrangements' filed with the petition: she and Bill agree that the children should continue to live with her, going to their present schools, and that they will continue to see Bill regularly. Mary and Bill have agreed to be flexible about Bill's contact with the children, rather than stick to a strict formula, say once a fortnight. In most cases the judge will approve the arrangements after reading the papers. If he is not entirely satisfied, he may ask for further information, or he may delay deciding until some outstanding difficulty has been resolved – for example, over housing. Or he may ask a court welfare officer to investigate the situation and make a report, or ask the divorcing couple to come to court for a personal interview. If the parents disagree about the arrangements for the children, and one or both want the court to decide, the district judge will give directions to make sure the dispute is resolved. In Bill and Mary's case this isn't necessary.

## Reaching agreement

Now the long-term financial arrangements can be sorted out. In many cases, a divorcing couple will decide these matters for themselves by negotiation rather than fight it out in court. Sometimes solicitors for the husband and wife will start negotiating the terms of the divorce settlement before the divorce petition is even filed. The petition itself may even be a bargaining counter in the negotiations. A wife who knows her husband wants to remarry quickly but has no grounds on which to divorce her may hold out for more money in return for agreeing to divorce him on the grounds of his adultery. Divorce has its elements of gamesmanship, just as much as any other branch of civil litigation.

Divorce gives the parties the right to make certain claims on each other and on the family assets. Unless the parties can agree on a settlement – which happens in most cases – the court will decide. Both husband and wife have equal right to claim, but in practice claims are usually made by the wife, since she usually earns less. A wife can ask, for example, for regular maintenance payments for herself, a share of the family home or the right to live in it, or a lump sum. Support for the children, if the parents don't agree or if the parent with care is on state benefits, will be worked out by an official body, the Child Support Agency.

State funding under the Community Legal Service, the successor to legal aid, is available to bring – or contest – any of these claims, as long as the financial criteria are met. But in most cases a couple will have to be assessed to see if their case is suitable for mediation first. If so, they will have to try mediation before they can apply for aid. Where mediation is unsuitable or breaks down, state funds will pay for a lawyer to negotiate a settlement and resolve disputes about children. Funding for a contested court case will usually be refused if a couple have not tried to settle the case without going to court, if the prospects of success are poor or borderline, or if the benefit to be achieved would not justify the cost of going to court. Divorce has been one of the biggest drains on the civil legal aid budget, and these tighter new criteria, together with funding for mediation, are designed to curb the cost of divorce disputes to the taxpayer.

Bill and Mary have managed to agree on their divorce and the arrangements for the children. The main sticking point is the house. Mary's earnings are low, but with her child benefit and the £400 a month Bill pays her for the children she's too well off to qualify for funding to sort out the long-term arrangements. However, she feels she needs a solicitor to safeguard her interests and decides she will have to find the money somehow.

In the event, agreement is reached without too much difficulty. Bill's solicitor persuades him that a court would be unlikely to order the house to be sold as long as the children needed a home. Mary's main concern is to have a secure home for herself and the children. She agrees to forgo any maintenance for herself if Bill transfers the family home to her. She will take a full-time job and pay the mortgage out of her earnings. Bill will continue to pay £200 a month for each of the two boys. The court is asked to approve the agreement and it is made into a court order.

Just as many claims in other areas of the civil law (like personal injuries) are settled out of court because the person liable knows he has to pay in any event and wants to avoid having to pay all the costs of an expensive trial as well, so most financial claims on divorce are settled by negotiation. Going to court and incurring large legal costs simply means there will a smaller cake left to divide.

Bill and Mary have opted for what is known as a clean break: a share-out of the family assets – often with the bigger share or possibly even the whole of the assets going to the wife – but no continuing obligation on the husband to maintain his ex-wife.

This is an option increasingly favoured in recent years by the courts and divorcing couples. The Matrimonial and Family Proceedings Act 1984 emphasizes the desirability of self-sufficiency for both ex-spouses if possible.

Most divorcing or separating parents reach their own agreements on maintenance for the children, but where the parent with care of the children – usually the mother – is living on state benefits, the case goes automatically to the Child Support Agency. This fixes the amount of support, currently by a complicated formula, soon to be replaced by a simple calculation based on a percentage of the absent parent's pay and the number of children. If parents reach their own agreement and this is made into a court order, only the court can increase or decrease it (though this too will change under new child support legislation – see p. 189). The exception is if the mother later loses her job and is thrown on to state benefits. Then the agency will automatically come on the scene and could increase the father's payments.

Bill's solicitor explains all this to him, but he still feels he wants to go for a clean break. Mary agrees. She wants to be self-supporting and the estate agency she works for has offered her a full-time job. Her mother, who lives nearby, has offered to collect the children from school every day and look after them till Mary comes home from work.

How does a divorcing couple reach a financial settlement? There are guidelines, based on what a court would order, just as there are guidelines for damages in accident cases. In divorce the sums are harder to do because of the court's wide discretion and all the factors that have to be weighed up: the length of the marriage, the contributions of the parties, whether there are children, the needs and responsibilities of the husband and wife in the future, any disabilities, and so on. In most cases, little weight if any is given to the conduct of the parties.

Both husband and wife have to disclose their earnings and assets and their expenses. The object of the exercise is to reach a settlement tailor-made for the particular couple while saving the cost, uncertainty and possibly bitterness of a court application. The court has a wide discretion in deciding what should happen to the home. It could be transferred outright to the wife as a quid pro quo for giving up her claim to maintenance or if the husband has flouted previous orders for maintenance. Other options are to award a proportion of the property's value to the wife and a proportion to the husband: half and half, or one-third/two-thirds, for example. If both will be able to rehouse themselves from the proceeds, the court may order the house to be sold. Often, where there are children, it will need to be kept as a home for them, and the husband may not be able to realize his share in it until the house is sold, possibly years later. But the court would want to be sure, before making this kind of order, that the husband had somewhere else to live. Sometimes the spouse who stays in the house is ordered to raise a mortgage to buy the other out. If the wife has no immediate plans to remarry but thinks she may remarry at some time in the future, she may forgo any claims to maintenance –

which ceases on remarriage – in favour of a lump sum or a larger share of the house, which she can keep even if she marries again. Courts must now take pension rights into account as well.

When a settlement is reached, lawyers advise that it should be drawn up as a 'consent order' to be approved by the court. It then takes effect as a court order, just as if it had been decided by the court after a full hearing. A court order may be worded so as to bar either party from any further court claims on the other. Without an order dismissing further claims, an ex-spouse could always come back and ask for more. If an open-ended order is made for weekly or monthly maintenance, either spouse can come back to the court later to ask for it to be increased or decreased. But property, once transferred, can't be transferred back, and a lump sum can be awarded only once.

## Fighting it out

If a couple can't agree on financial terms, then either spouse – husband or wife, petitioner or respondent – can make an application to the court. In practice, almost all applications are made by wives, although the law makes no distinction. Wives are rarely ordered to maintain their husbands, but they may be ordered by the Child Support Agency to pay something towards the upkeep of children living with their father, and husbands have been awarded large lump sums in a few cases.

Many millions of pounds in public funds are spent each year on wrangles between divorcing spouses over money, property and children. State funding can be a powerful bargaining counter, particularly if held by only one party to the contest. Many more wives than husbands qualify, and wives can use the threat of legal proceedings to wangle a bigger share of the cake. A few bitter wives will refuse all reasonable offers, determined to put the spouse who has 'wronged' them to the maximum expense and inconvenience. On the other hand, some husbands see no reason why they should continue to pay for a wife they are no longer getting the benefit of, and will try to hide their assets or dispose of them, and thwart maintenance claims by refusing to work.

## Money and property

Most divorce petitions include a 'prayer' asking for maintenance, property and so on – usually, in fact, asking for the whole range of possible orders. This is almost always thrown in even if the petitioner has no intention of making any claims at all, 'just in case'. The petitioner who fails to ask for an order in the petition has an extra step to go through if she later wants to pursue her claim: she will have to ask the court's permission to go ahead with her application. As long as the application is there on the record, though not proceeded with, a husband is never entirely safe from a claim by an ex-wife, even if he has heard nothing from her for years. And maintenance orders, once made, can be varied up or down, as the circumstances of either party changes. For instance, if the husband takes on the responsibility of supporting a new family or the wife moves in with another man, the husband can apply to have his ex-wife's maintenance payments reduced. On the other hand, if the wife has to stop working because of illness, or the husband gets a big salary increase, she can apply for bigger payments. However, the court can also rule that there should be a clean break and a wife's payments should stop, either immediately or after a period of time. The court can award a lump sum only once, and whatever is decided about the family home will stand. There is no question of coming back years later and asking the court to change its mind, though if one party thinks the court has made a wrong order an appeal against it is possible within a reasonable time.

You won't be able to get a lump sum or share of property if you remarry before you make your application, but the usual step of including the application in the petition will save you from that pitfall. Remarrying before the court hears the application won't prevent you from getting something, but it might affect the amount. If you're the respondent – the spouse who didn't petition for divorce – and you want to remarry before the finances are sorted out, you should put in an application for financial provision to the court first.

Hearings are in private and nobody not connected with the case is allowed to attend. Under a new procedure piloted in 1999–2000, and due to be introduced throughout England and Wales in June 2000, husband and wife each have to complete a detailed financial question-naire. The aim is to bring all the financial information out at the beginning, and to concentrate the parties' minds on the areas of dispute. At a pre-hearing, any settlement offers which have been made must be disclosed to the district judge, who will indicate what will happen at the final hearing. The intention is that more cases should be settled before the final hearing, rather than at the doors of the court, which often happened in the past.

If the district judge has to make the decision, he will weigh up all the factors, but the result will come down to the amount of money and property available to be shared out, and the needs of the two ex-spouses and their children.

In deciding what a husband can afford to pay, the court looks at all the circumstances – including the fact that he has a second wife or live-in girlfriend. If Bill and Mary had fought over maintenance, the earnings of Bill's girlfriend, Jane, would have been weighed up in the scales. This is not done by any crude mathematical formula – the court will not, for example, just lump Bill's and Jane's incomes together. The fact that Jane is self-supporting and contributing to expenses simply means that Bill can pay more than he otherwise might. But the end result, many second wives argue, is that they are forced to work to keep their husbands' first wives.

Child support payments – assessed by the Child Support Agency where the parent caring for the children is on state benefits or where the parents can't agree – will depend on the absent parent's income and that of the parent with care of the child. If the absent parent is earning little, the payments could be virtually nothing, while fathers on substantial incomes are ordered to pay considerable sums. Under changes expected to be implemented by late 2001, even if parents agree on the amount of child support and have it incorporated in a court order, after 12 months either parent will be entitled to apply to the CSA for the amount to be changed.

In deciding what should happen to the family home, the main consideration is the welfare of any children under 18. The courts have said that both parents should have a home so that the children can visit and stay with their father, if the finances can be stretched to two homes. Because whoever has the children is usually allowed to stay in the home, fights ostensibly over which parent the children should live with may actually be about the right to live in the family home.

The home will not often be transferred outright to one spouse. The wife, if she has the children, may be allowed to live in the house until the children finish their education, after which the house will be sold and the proceeds divided. If this solution would be likely to leave the wife in her middle-age without enough to buy another house, the court may decide to let her stay in the house for life, or until she remarries. If the couple are young and childless, the house may be sold and the money split. Or one spouse may be ordered to raise a lump sum to buy the other out. The court has a wide discretion. The legal ownership of the home counts for little.

## The children

Most parents manage to agree on which parent the child should live with. Contact with the children by the absent parent is a much more fruitful battleground. Some cases go on for years, with endless court applications and arguments over contact, running up thousands of pounds in bills in the process. The overriding factor the court will look to in reaching any decision about children is: what is in the child's best interests? Judges usually rely on the reports of court welfare officers, who visit both parents in their homes, often talk to the children and visit their schools, and make recommendations to the court.

Continuing contact between the children and their absent parent is clearly an emotional problem rather than a legal one, and the law offers no really effective remedy to the father whose ex-wife denies him contact. A mother who refuses to comply with a contact order can be sent to prison for contempt of court, but judges are reluctant to jail mothers in these cases. However, judges have recently been taking a stronger line with recalcitrant mothers and a few have been jailed for defying contact orders.

Mediation is a development which has taken some of the sting out of clashes over children of divorce. Mediation services have been set up around the country to help divorcing parents resolve their grievances instead of perpetuating them through fights over their children, and most courts bring warring spouses together with a divorce court welfare officer to see if they can be helped to work out their own arrangements for the children. Under the new funding code for the Community Legal Service, which has replaced legal aid, most applicants for funding for a court fight over children (or other matters) will first have to have their case assessed to see if it is suitable for mediation. If it is deemed suitable and the applicant refuses to try mediation, funding will generally be refused.

A growing number of lawyers are also trained as mediators and will help couples work out a complete agreement jointly, including a financial and property settlement. This allows couples to avoid months of costly negotiations between opposing solicitors, although both parties are advised to have the agreement vetted by their own separate solicitors.

## The future

Mediation is likely to be the means by which many divorcing couples sort out disputes over children, money and property in the future. No-fault divorce is not now on the horizon, since the government has decided not to bring into force the part of the Family Law Act which would have introduced it. It may re-emerge in the future, but probably not in the form envisaged in the Act.

CHAPTER IX

# The Price of Justice

The solicitor was explaining his charges to a new client. 'My charging rate is £150 an hour,' he said. The client leapt up and bolted for the door, pausing only to call over his shoulder: 'I would have said goodbye, only I can't afford to.'

Fear of the cost is one of the most powerful deterrents to using lawyers' services. Even if a client overcomes his initial fear and gets across the threshold of a solicitor's office, he worries about how the costs are mounting up, as the invisible taxi meter ticks away. Are clients' anxieties about costs justified? Do solicitors overcharge, and are there any controls on their charges? The Royal Commission on Legal Services, which reported in 1979, looked at the whole question of lawyers' fees, and came to the conclusion that they were not too high for the work done. But they thought that the legal processes themselves – particularly in conveyancing and litigation – should be simplified, with a view to reducing delay and cost. In recent years, competition and price advertising have slashed conveyancing charges. Complex and time-consuming procedures still price civil litigation beyond the pockets of many, and successive governments have cut back dramatically on the numbers eligible to have their litigation funded by the state. But two recent developments hold out hope of making litigation more affordable by ordinary people. The Woolf reforms to the civil justice system came into effect in 1999 with the aim of making litigation simpler, cheaper and quicker. Early indications are encouraging. The second development, conditional fees – known colloquially as no-win, no-fee – allows middle income earners previously priced out of the courts the chance to litigate with little or no financial risk.

## Lawyers' charges

For a solicitor, time is money. In most firms, every solicitor, legal executive and trainee solicitor has an hourly expense rate, based on his share of the firm's expenses, including his salary (or a notional salary if he is a partner). The expense rate represents the actual cost to the firm of doing the work, not including any profit. But the hourly rate the solicitor actually charges the client – the 'charging rate' or 'charge-out rate' will include a profit element as well.

Because the rates are related to the firm's expenses, firms with lower overheads can charge less than practices paying high rents and salaries. Overheads in the average practice eat up about two-thirds of the fees earned. A solicitor practising from home will be able to charge considerably lower rates than a large firm renting expensive city-centre offices and paying high salaries. And a firm in central London will charge more than a practice in a small market town in Lincolnshire or Wales. Charge-out rates also vary according to the type of work and the size of the firm, with the larger firms charging higher rates. The Law Society's autumn 1998 survey shows typical rates for partners doing personal injury work – accident compensation cases – ranging from £106 an hour for a sole practitioner to £170 for a partner in a firm of 26–80 partners.

The size of the bill which eventually lands on the client's doormat may depend not only on the time spent on the job, but also on such factors as the skill and knowledge and effort involved, the value of any property dealt with, and the importance of the matter to the client. A transaction which involves a great deal of money may justify a higher fee than one where less money is at risk, but which takes the same length of time.

In the past, conveyancing fees subsidized the less profitable litigation work. Now, fierce competition among solicitors for conveyancing work has pared profits and led to a more streamlined service with fewer frills. Many solicitors will charge a flat rate for conveyancing regardless of the price of the house or flat, and most will quote a fee in advance.

## Court proceedings

In cases where court proceedings may be necessary, solicitors are unlikely to be able to commit themselves to a firm price in advance, because the way in which a case will progress is to a large extent out of their control. So much depends on how easy or difficult it is to persuade the other side to co-operate. A few letters back and forth may be sufficient. Or the case may go to a full trial, or a settlement may only happen at the door of the court.

But solicitors are obliged by professional rules to inform clients in advance about the basis on which they will charge. This could be a fixed fee, hourly rates, or some other variation. If no firm figure is possible, the solicitor can give an estimate or forecast, but must make it clear that it is not a firm quotation. The estimate could be, for example, 'not more than £x, including VAT and disbursements'. If it looks as though the estimate will be exceeded, the client must be informed. Often, unless a client is being funded by the state or under a no-win, no-fee agreement, solicitors will ask for a down payment at the beginning of the case, a sum 'on account of costs', as they call it. As the case progresses, most solicitors deliver interim bills – showing how the money in hand has been spent – and ask for further sums on account. A client who is convicted of a criminal offence, or who loses his case or abandons it, is not likely to regard his solicitor's bill as a matter of high priority, so the prudent solicitor likes to cover most of his costs as he goes along. This practice also keeps the client from running up an enormous bill without his knowledge. If he prefers, a client can authorize the solicitor to incur costs only up to a certain amount – say, £1000. When the limit is reached, the solicitor will have to seek approval before doing any more work. Alternatively, the client can ask for an account every month, showing where he stands.

Costs include solicitors' fees, 'disbursements' – out-of-pocket expenses such as court fees, payments to doctors and other expert witnesses, barristers' fees – and VAT. Medical specialists may charge as much as £1000 or £1500 for a written report, and most charge between £75 and £150 an hour for going to court. A consultant engineer, who may be asked for an opinion on how a road accident happened, is likely to charge around £75 to £100 per hour.

Barristers' fees are more variable than solicitors' charges. Though top specialists can command high rates for advisory work, fees for pre-trial paperwork are on the whole not high. The fees for trial work, however, make up for the underpayment on the paperwork. In the more difficult case, using a QC and junior barrister, the client is paying for the constant attendance of three lawyers – the QC, the junior and the solicitor or his representative.

If a case goes to court, barristers are entitled to a 'brief fee', to cover preparation plus the first day of the trial, and a daily sum, called a 'refresher'. A QC in a High Court accident case can usually expect a minimum brief fee of £5000 plus refreshers of £1000 a day, a junior around half as much. (Though if the barristers and solicitors are both working on a no-win, no-fee basis (*see* p. 201) both will receive nothing if they lose and their normal fees plus an uplift if they win.) Not surprisingly, few personal injury cases get as far as court. The vast majority are settled out of court before the court costs are incurred. One side's costs for five days in the High Court on a contested personal injury case, with a QC, can run to £50,000 to £70,000, including the solicitors' preparation.

Barristers' charges vary hugely. A raw barrister handling a guilty plea in the magistrates' court will count himself lucky to get £40, while top commercial silks can command brief fees of £200,000 plus refreshers of up to £3000 a day for lengthy, complicated cases.

Pressures to settle out of court are strong. A trial can easily double the costs on both sides. But our legal system puts an extra hazard in the litigant's path: the danger that he might end up paying both sides' costs. In litigation the usual rule is that the loser pays the winner's costs – or most of them – as well as his own. Where cases are settled out of court, the party who pays up usually has to agree to pay his opponent's costs as well.

## Challenging a bill

The winner's solicitor's bill, payable by the loser, may be assessed by the court or (more usually) the amount will just be agreed, if the loser's solicitor thinks it looks reasonable. Agreeing the bill saves time and the assessment fee which would have to be paid to the court.

A client dissatisfied with his own solicitor's bill should raise it first with the solicitor. Not only do professional rules oblige solicitors to give clients detailed advance information on costs, but firms must also have a machinery for dealing with complaints, including those over costs. If this does not resolve the matter, the client can have the bill assessed by the court, though few clients do because the process is complicated and can be expensive. The bill need not be for court work: it could be for conveyancing or any other legal work. If the bill is reduced by one-fifth or more, the solicitor will have to pay the fee for having the costs assessed by the court. If not, the client has to pay.

A far better and more usual way of challenging the fairness of a solicitor's bill – because there is no risk that the client will end up paying more – is to ask the solicitor to apply to the Law Society for a 'remuneration certificate'. This procedure is available for conveyancing, probate, commercial work, leases, tax advice and most other types of legal work. But it cannot be used if the work involves court proceedings: for example, defending someone against a criminal charge, petitioning for divorce, applying for maintenance, suing someone or being sued. In these cases assessment by the court is the only resort.

To seek a remuneration certificate, all the client has to do is ask the solicitor to set the wheels in motion, though the client must act quickly to meet the time limits, and the solicitor is entitled to ask for part of the bill to be paid first. If he refuses to apply for a certificate, he can be reported for a breach of professional conduct. Filling in the application and sending his file off to the Office for the Supervision of Solicitors (OSS) puts him to a lot of trouble, so he may knock a bit off the bill to save himself the time and effort.

The OSS may first attempt to resolve the dispute by conciliation between solicitor and client. If this doesn't work, staff will look at all the files, see what work has been done, decide whether the charges are reasonable, and issue a provisional certificate either upholding the charge or reducing it to a fair level. If the parties don't accept the provisional certificate, the case goes to a committee, which will issue a formal certificate reducing the bill or confirming it as reasonable. The review is free to the client and there is no chance of having the bill increased rather than reduced.

The OSS is concerned mainly with whether the work done justifies the fees, but a solicitor who does an unnecessary amount of work on what should have been a straightforward job will find his fees marked down. And one who does a really bad job won't get the rate for a good job: in extreme cases he might get nothing at all. Failing to inform the client about the likely cost of the case could lead to a reduced bill, even if the charges are considered reasonable.

# State funding for legal help

Legal aid, introduced in 1950, was conceived as the second prong of the welfare state, the legal equivalent of the National Health Service, created two years earlier. A fund was set up, controlled by the Lord Chancellor, to pay lawyers in private practice to undertake litigation for those of 'small and moderate means', along with their privately paid work. The work would be done in just the same way, but in the end the costs would be paid by the government, rather than the client, but on a slightly lower scale. In 1972 a separate Legal Advice and Assistance Scheme (the 'green form scheme') was set up to cover legal advice and help, short of court proceedings. Civil legal aid paid for most types of cases in the county court, High Court and appeal courts. Fights between ex-spouses over money, property and children, and accident cases, were the two biggest categories, but civil legal aid covered any dispute involving a civil court except libel and slander actions. When it was introduced, it was intended to help people of 'small or moderate means' enforce their rights. But through the 1980s the cost of the scheme rocketed, partly fuelled by the rise in the divorce rate. In an attempt to curb the costs of the service, which was demand led, the government let the numbers qualifying for aid drop by failing to increase eligibility levels in line with inflation. The bulk of the population, the middle-income group, were too well off for legal aid but not nearly rich enough to afford major litigation.

In the mid-1990s the Conservative Lord Chancellor, Lord Mackay, started laying plans for a radical restructuring of legal aid. Although it was a godsend for people who could not afford to pay lawyers' fees, the existing scheme had many flaws. It was targeted on remedies through the courts, when many of the areas most important to ordinary people – jobs, welfare benefits, immigration – were dealt with by tribunals. It was lawyer-led and focused on legal fields that lawyers chose to deal with – personal injury, family law and crime rather than welfare benefits and debt. Any solicitor could handle a legal aid case, so most cases were not handled by specialists. Too many unmeritorious cases were funded because the lawyer who stood to get the work (and be paid, win or lose) rated the chances of success too optimistically. And there were few controls on lawyers' bills, which were based largely on hourly and daily rates and were assessed case by case by the courts after the case was concluded. In the mid-to-late 1990s, the top QCs doing legal aid work could earn £300,000 or more in a good year.

Lord Mackay's plans were taken up and developed further by the new Lord Chancellor, Lord Irvine, after Labour came to power in 1997. Franchises were granted to specialist lawyers and by August 1999 only specialists were allowed to handle clinical negligence cases. The Lord Chancellor announced in 1997 that legal aid would be withdrawn from ordinary personal injury cases – though not medical negligence cases, at least for the time being – a step taken in April 2000. Except for the very high cost cases, these will have to be handled henceforth by solicitors on a no-win, no-fee basis.

As of April 2000, state funding for civil litigation, advice and help is no longer termed 'legal aid'. It will operate in a radically different way. The Legal Aid Board, which administered the civil legal aid scheme, has been replaced by a Legal Services Commission. The Commission provides funding for legal information, advice, help and representation through the new Community Legal Service.

Under the legal aid scheme, any solicitors' firm could take on any legal aid case and claim payment afterwards from the state. Under the new system, only those with proven expertise will provide publicly funded help and representation. The government has developed a contracting system under which only those who meet quality controls and are awarded contracts will be able to provide the service. The move is expected to be completed in April 2001.

The aim of the CLS is to target funds mainly on the less well off. But the plan is to extend information and advice to a wider cross-section of the community in local areas where local authorities agree to provide funding of their own. The service will be provided through contracts with local solicitors, Citizens' Advice Bureaux, advice agencies, and law centres. Local areas will set local priorities but the CLS as a whole will give high priority to certain types of cases – those involving children, housing, and cases with a wider public interest: those which could benefit a larger group, not just the individual involved in the case.

The budget for state legal help will be capped for the first time. Tough new criteria will apply to claims for compensation and other money claims under a new funding code. Under the legal aid scheme, the cost of the litigation could eclipse the size of the damages; the new funding code is designed to prevent this. A cost/benefit analysis will be carried out, based on the prospects of success, the amount of the likely damages, and the likely cost of the case. To get state funding for a case with an 80 per cent chance of success, the applicant will have to show that damages are likely to exceed the costs. With a 60–80 per cent likelihood of success, the potential damages will have to be twice as large as the costs. And where the chances of success are only 50–60 per cent, likely damages will have to exceed costs by 4 : 1.

It will be easier to get funding for high priority areas – challenges to the decisions of public bodies, cases which raise human rights issues, cases alleging wrongdoing by the police and other authorities, housing and social welfare cases, child welfare and domestic violence cases. Medical negligence cases will still be funded, subject to the cost/benefit analysis, but funding will not be available for most personal injury claims, which will be left for lawyers to take on a no-win, no-fee basis.

But the CLS may cover the cost of investigation to see whether a case has a good chance of success, if this is likely to be expensive. Cases which are more costly than usual to run may qualify for help with court costs and barristers' fees. Group claims, such as actions by a number of people injured by the same faulty drug, or in a rail crash or other disaster, may get funding for the overall investigative work, but not for the individual claims, which will have to be done under no-win, no-fee deals.

Divorce battles consumed a large chunk of the budget under the old legal aid scheme. The new scheme aims to cut down on court fights by targeting funding on the types of legal help designed to promote early settlements. The fund will pay for lawyers to provide advice to clients going through mediation – a process whereby the parties try to resolve their own dispute with the help of a neutral third party – and, with some exceptions, divorce-court battles will not be funded unless mediation is attempted first and fails. Funding will also cover lawyers' work in getting disclosure of the other side's assets, as a preliminary to negotiating a settlement.

Mediation for cases other than divorce or family disputes, as an alternative to litigation, can also be funded from the Community Legal Service Fund. The government favours more use of the various types of alternative dispute resolution (ADR) as a cheaper and speedier way of resolving disputes than going to court.

## Beyond state funding

Litigants who enter the law machine can expose themselves to substantial financial risks. The outcome of litigation is uncertain, and those who lose usually face a double whammy – a bill for the other side's costs as well as their own, under the 'loser pays' rule. The Americans have long had a method of paying their lawyers which allows them to litigate without the fear of substantial loss. Lawyers can take on a case on a no-win, no-fee basis. If they win, they get a percentage of the damages, usually around a third, but sometimes more. If they lose, they get nothing. Levels of damages decided by juries in the USA are much higher than in England, where judges are responsible for fixing awards. So the winner is still left with a respectable sum, even after the lawyer's rake-off.

English lawyers have traditionally been forbidden to take cases on this basis. But the ban was removed in 1995 for a few types of cases, most significantly for personal injury cases. In 1998, the Lord Chancellor extended no-win, no-fee deals – technically known as conditional fee agreements (CFAs) – to all types of civil cases apart from divorce. Under CFAs lawyers are not allowed to claim a percentage share of the damages as their reward (as US lawyers can do). But they can agree with the client in advance to be paid an uplift on their normal fee if they win the case. The size of the uplift or 'success fee' – between nothing and 100 per cent – will depend on the lawyer's assessment of how risky the case is. Would-be litigants can shop around to find the lawyer offering the best deal. The Law Society recommended that the fee the lawyer eventually takes, including the uplift, should not exceed 25 per cent of the damages won, and this 'cap' has become standard. Some critics argue that a 100 per cent uplift is too much. (It was increased from 10 per cent and then 20 per cent after solicitors warned that such small uplifts would not be enough to persuade them to take the risk of losing and getting nothing.) Some lawyers say that even a 100 per cent uplift is not enough to persuade them to take on difficult or complex cases.

No-win, no-fee deals work better in the US system, where each party to litigation bears his own costs. They cannot achieve the purpose of eliminating financial risk under the English 'loser pays' rule. The rule could be abolished, but it seems unfair that someone forced to take court action to get compensation should have his damages reduced by the cost of forcing the person at fault to pay up.

The insurance industry came up with a solution. For a premium, the client is insured against losing and having to pay the other side's costs. The premium depends on the amount of costs covered and the chances of success.

Lawyers were bitterly opposed to the idea that CFAs should replace legal aid for personal injury cases. The government gave the profession and the insurance industry a transitional period to make sure the plan would work. Early evidence suggests that it is broadly succeeding and is boosting access to the law for the middle income group, who would not, in any event, have qualified for legal aid.

Research by Stella Yarrow of Westminster University for the Policy Studies Institute in 1997 showed that within 18 months of their introduction, CFAs for personal injury cases had become established among specialist solicitors. The study dispelled fears that solicitors would automatically set the uplift on their fees at 100 per cent. The average uplift was 43 per cent, and only one in 10 cases had an uplift between 90 and 100 per cent. Solicitors seemed a little uncertain about risk assessment and in a number of cases had applied uplifts which were too high or too low in relation to the risk. Further research in 1999 by Stella Yarrow and Pamela Abrams, this time focusing on clients' experience, found that those who signed up to no-win, no-fee deals had little understanding of how they operated and did not shop around for the best deal. But most said they would not have been able to pursue their case without a CFA.

When the government unveiled the plan to remove legal aid from 'ordinary' personal injury cases, with a threat (still unfulfilled) to withdraw aid from clinical negligence cases in due course, lawyers insisted that CFAs were a non-starter for medical cases, with their high initial costs of investigation and uncertain outcome. Clients would not be able to afford the £2000 or £3000 it would take to instruct an expert and find out whether they had a good case. The insurers would either turn them down or charge a premium way beyond the client's pocket, the lawyers argued. But specialist solicitors are finding that insurers, who have their own panels to vet cases, are taking them on. Premiums are high, but the insurers have developed new products which allow the client to postpone payment of the premium and disbursements – out of pocket expenses such as experts' fees – and pay them only if and when the case is won. It is now possible to bring a claim without having to incur any expenditure upfront. A further development, which came into force in April 2000, allows litigants who win their cases on CFAs to get not only their solicitors' normal costs and disbursements from the loser, but the uplift and the premium as well. As an alternative to CFAs, policies are available to insure litigants against their own solicitors' costs and disbursements as well as their opponent's. The solicitor is paid normal fees, but no uplift, win or lose.

Barristers may operate in one of two ways under CFAs – they may work, like solicitors, on a no-win, no-fee basis, or they may be treated as a disbursement, getting paid normal fees whether they win or lose. As CFAs become an established way of conducting litigation, barristers will come under more and more pressure to take the same risks as solicitors.

Insurance to cover a proposed court case is known as 'after the event' insurance. Another type, 'before-the-event', is taken out not to fund a particular piece of litigation, but to insure against the eventuality of ever becoming involved in litigation. Developed before 'after the event' insurance was ever thought of, this type of legal expenses insurance is popular in Germany but has never caught on in the UK, except as an add-on to motor or home contents insurance, or as group cover for employees or clubs. Many people have limited cover in this fashion, often without even being aware of it.

## State-funded criminal defence

Survey after survey has shown that defendants without a lawyer to represent them at their trial are more likely to be convicted (sometimes wrongly) and, if convicted, to get a stiffer sentence than they would otherwise have got. The lawyer knows his way around the procedure of the court, how best to present a case, what points to raise, what questions to ask. Quite often he can mean the difference between conviction and acquittal, because he sees a defence to the charge which would not occur to a lay person.

Criminal legal aid is meant to ensure that, where the interests of justice demand it, a person charged with a criminal offence should have legal representation. To qualify for legal aid, a defendant has to show two things: first, that he cannot afford to pay for a lawyer himself, and second, that he needs a lawyer. The system does not assume that everyone charged with a criminal offence should have legal representation. It has to be in the interests of justice for him to have it. This is decided by the court, based on guidelines laying down the circumstances in which legal aid should be granted. Some of the guidelines deal with special cases, such as language difficulties, or the fact that a complex point of law is involved or expert cross-examination is needed. But the most important rule says that legal aid should be granted whenever there is a serious risk that the defendant may lose his liberty or his job.

Over 95 per cent of defendants in the Crown Court, where the more serious charges are dealt with, are financed by legal aid. The costs of defending a serious charge are so high that very few defendants are able to meet them from their own pockets, and it is unquestionably in the interests of justice that someone charged with a serious crime – where the resources of the state are ranged against him – should have legal representation. In the magistrates' court, by contrast, many defendants are unrepresented. Some don't apply for legal aid; others do and are turned down.

An important factor in the outcome of a criminal case is the quality of the legal help provided. A four-year study of nearly 50 law firms in England and Wales, headed by Michael McConville of Warwick University (published in 1993), found that criminal defence solicitors routinely processed legal aid clients into guilty pleas rather than exploring the possibility of a defence. While some firms provided a good service, others undertook no independent investigative work and treated their clients as 'economic units' to be processed through the system.

From April 2001, a new Criminal Defence Service (CDS) will replace the system under which any law firm could do criminal legal aid work and claim fees according to the work done. Most publicly-funded criminal defence work will continue to be done by firms in private practice, but only by those with contracts with the Legal Services Commission. Only firms which meet quality standards will be given contracts, and the system will allow tighter control on costs. The CDS will also be able to use salaried public defenders to some extent, a system which has been piloted in Scotland but never before used in England and Wales.

# Index